PERSPECTIVES

AND THE

CONSTRUCTION

OF CONSCIOUSNESS

ALSO BY ANTON G. HARDY

Psychology and the Critical Revolution

PERSPECTIVES AND THE CONSTRUCTION OF CONSCIOUSNESS

The Phenomenological Alternative

ANTON G. HARDY

JAMES PUBLICATIONS
Box 545
GUILDERLAND • NEW YORK • 12084

Published by
James Publications
Box 545
Guilderland, New York
SAN 695-1783

© by Anton G. Hardy

ISBN 0-9615267-1-8

Library of Congress Control Number: 2006907219

Printed and bound in the United States of America

IN MEMORY OF

DAVID HARDY

WHO COLLABORATED WITH ME

IN THE WRITING

CONTENTS

PERSPECTIVES

AND THE

CONSTRUCTION

OF CONSCIOUSNESS

The Phenomenological Alternative

INTRODUCTION

*"After all, mind is such an odd predicament
for matter to get into. I often marvel how
something like hydrogen, the simplest atom,
forged in some early chaos of the universe,
could lead to us and the gorgeous fever we
call consciousness."*
—Ackerman, *The Moon by Whale Light*

1

When we look at the intellectual landscape that surrounds us today, we find that two large subject areas are resistant to our understanding. One of these is consciousness. Consciousness is a central fact of our human functioning; it is the seat of all our awareness-of-things, the domain in which we see what we see, think what we think, imagine what we imagine. Despite a recent plethora of books on this topic, however, it remains essentially inscrutable. It withstands every attempt we make at essential penetration.

The other area that is resistant to our understanding is creativity. So common in our intellectual landscape that we tend to ignore it, the creative presents itself in the ever-fresh expressions of painters and architects, the original compositions of musicians and writers, the new concepts and theories of philosophers

1

and scientists. It is seen in our practical life as well when, confronted by a breakdown in a vehicle or mechanical appliance, say, we need to find some solution. Creativity is an irrepressible feature of our human functioning. Yet in its essential nature, its manner of operating, the creative process itself persists in its impenetrability.

Beyond this, however, we find that the entire realm of the "human" is vexed. Psychology, the discipline that is most directly devoted to acquiring a knowledge of the human being, has been beset with unexpected difficulties. Split from early on between those who straightforwardly engage its subject in pursuit of clinical understanding and those who make of it an object for measurement, it has fragmented even further into various areas, approaches and schools (Hardy 1988). And other human sciences suffer from this fragmentation as well: sociology and anthropology, history and political science, economics and humanistic studies all divide between those who focus on the values and meanings of the human being as these are exhibited in various activities and settings, and those who pursue their understanding through rigorous methodology. In their attempts to gain a meaningful understanding of their human subject, these disciplines are unaccountably thwarted; they seem unable to find a path that will lead them to knowledge that is at once significant *and* dependable.

A serious problem confronts us, then, in regard to the human. Why should these disciplines be so stymied in their efforts? Why should such subjects as consciousness and creativity be so resistant to our understanding? The roots of this problem reach down, I believe, to our most fundamental assumptions: they originate in beliefs that are so ingrained in us that they "make common sense." Together, these assumptions and these beliefs form a general paradigm that for centuries has governed our thinking. They stem from the philosophical system that is commonly referred to as "Realism."

In broad outline, Realism establishes two fundamental postulates. It asserts that there is a reality out there that is independent of us and our activities, and in addition, a copy function that brings this reality into our minds. With these assumptions, then, it is able to resolve such important problems as how we come by the contents we have in our mind and how we can agree with each other on what is "there." But it has also encountered difficulties. In the course of its long history, it has given rise to various paradoxes, contradictions, and confusions that no amount of philosophical theorizing has been able to resolve. One of these is a resolute bias in favor of the "physical." And it is this bias that impedes our efforts to understand the human.

If we are to be more successful in these efforts, then, we must seek another paradigm. We must search for a different set of principles upon which to base our understanding. And it will be to this task that I apply myself in this book: in the following, I will attempt to bring into formulation a paradigm that can replace Realism and that can lead us through the difficulties that are contingent upon its standpoint. This will be a

paradigm, fortunately, that need not be brought forth
ex nihilo; in philosophy's long and productive history,
important elements of it have already come to expression. My task will be limited, therefore, to picking up
these elements and weaving them together: I will
attempt to find the thread that, running through them,
makes of them a coherent whole.

2

The journey will begin with the great "Copernican
revolution" of Immanuel Kant. In 1781, Kant broke
with the Realistic tradition by pointing out that the
Dingen an sich of its "reality" are totally beyond our
reach; the "things in themselves" lie outside any possibility of our "having," of being directly grasped. Any
statements we make in regard to them, therefore, are
unverifiable. And instead of being concerned with
these outside things, we must turn to what is accessi-
ble to us, the *representations* of these things that we
have in our experience. Thus, it is experience that
must serve as the ground of our knowledge. Instead of
trying to find out how things actually "are," we must
turn our focus to how we "know" them to be; and our
ultimate questions must concern the conditions that
make it possible for experience to "be."

Kant thus introduced into philosophy an entirely
different direction. And this was a direction that was
phenomenological in its orientation, that took as its
focus the "phenomena" of experience. More than a
century later, Edmund Husserl secured this direction
further with his concept of a "phenomenological

reduction." He gave explicit recognition to the fact that our primary data are always of a phenomenological kind, are always "in consciousness." By the early part of the last century, therefore, essential elements of the phenomenological outlook had been laid down.

Advance after Husserl, however, became difficult. As Martin Heidegger, Maurice Merleau-Ponty and others, tried to follow in his footsteps, they failed to reach the goal of a complete and comprehensive system. Their conceptions were often unclear; their writing was obscure. And as the century progressed, the phenomenological movement gradually lost steam. It became less and less a focus of philosophical thinking, and was overshadowed by other, non-phenomenological orientations.

In retrospect, we are able to see that a major impediment for these early phenomenologists was their inability to break completely with Realism. Dedicated as they were to introducing into philosophy a fresh new approach, they nevertheless succumbed to the ontological imperative. Husserl, for instance, proposed a transcendental subjectivity that was "an absolute source." Heidegger became preoccupied with the vicissitudes of "Being." And in their discussions of "the world," phenomenologists in general failed to distinguish unambiguously between a world that was *ontological reality* and a world that was *phenomenologically in consciousness*.

Another path had been taken, however, in response to Kant's revolution. Not as well known, this was the direction developed by neo-Kantians, notably those who belonged to the Marburg school. These thinkers gave full recognition to the radical import of Kant's revolution; in contrast to these phenomenologists, they hewed closely to Kant's "critical" rule that one avoid in one's explanations any reliance upon a "reality" or "Being," any recourse to the "transcendental." This path came to culmination in Ernst Cassirer's great "philosophy of symbolic forms": here, a comprehensive system was advanced that encompassed the entire range of human activity from myth to mathematics, from religion to science, from language to art. All these enterprises, Cassirer proposed, stem from a fundamental activity: they are the products of a key *symbolic function*.

As I attempt in the following to continue with the phenomenological program, then, I will rely upon this second path. It is here, I believe, that we will find the consistency of approach and precision of conceptualization that is needed to achieve this program's goals. What we will see emerging, then, will be an exciting new outlook, a vista that opens upon an entirely different landscape. Instead of being under the sway of an importunate "objective," this landscape will be *humanly* oriented; it will have as its focus whatever appears in human experience. *And among these appearances, now, will be this objective itself! They will include the perceptions and thoughts that put before us a physical "reality."*

3

The new paradigm will include in its corpus, then, elements that are fundamental in Realism. Still, the tenacity of Realism's paradigm is not to be underestimated. Although it has been subjected in recent years to increasingly acute criticism—although it has been challenged in this postmodern era in regard, in particular, to its espousal of this very "authoritative objective"—it retains its hegemony. Its postulation of an external reality satisfies our need for something that is solid, something in which we can anchor ourselves. And as long as there is no real alternative to turn to—no paradigm of equal scope and comprehensiveness—the tendency to slide back into it will over and over reassert itself.

In order to avoid this fate, then, I will need to go down to our most fundamental conceptions. I will need—with apologies to René Descartes and other philosophical groundbreakers—to "begin at the beginning." Husserl himself attempted just this: in his and his followers' efforts "to describe phenomena . . . whatever appears in the manner in which it appears" (Moran 2000, 4), they issued the rallying cry, "Back to the things themselves!" They attempted to identify what was fundamental in human experience, what was pure and underived. In doing so, however, they failed to sufficiently analyze just what these "things" were: Did they consist in individual percepts such as are given in our everyday experience? Were they those simple concepts like "tree," "animal," and "star" that are so influential in our outlook on things? Or were they some kind of further element that had yet to be defined?[1]

The fact is that careful consideration of the elements of consciousness—our "phenomena"—show them in every case to be *perspectives*. Whether perceptual or conceptual in nature, they possess this unique kind of *perspectival structure*. And far from being "pure," they hold within them both a subjective standpoint from which something is being viewed and an object which then becomes visible from this standpoint. They thus trail with them all the factors that go into this subjective position. Implied in each phenomenon when it is a visible "thing," for instance, is the particular spatial location we are occupying at the moment; and implied in this and every other kind of phenomenon—in anything at all, in fact, that we "have"—are the innate expectations we are harboring at the moment, the cultural forces that have conditioned our way of viewing in general, and the personal biases and predilections that we have developed along the way. "Perspective," therefore, moves into central position in my discussion: it will be the door that opens for us the domain of consciousness.

We are already accustomed to the fact, of course, that we often operate from perspectives. In our daily life, we use such phrases as "from my point of view," "this, of course, is only the way I see things," "it is my opinion that . . . ." We speak of "gaining perspective," of "taking an alternative view," of "approaching things differently."

But hidden within this usage is a hornet's nest of questions. Are we willing to say, for instance, that perspectives are *all* that we have? Are we prepared to go so far as to say that we are *imprisoned* in these perspectives, that we are irretrievably confined to just one-sided views of things? And if so, what then of the reality? Can this seep in somehow amidst these one-sided views, informing us of the way things actually are?

If this does happen, however, how do we recognize it? By what criteria does reality announce itself and enable us to distinguish it from what are, now, "mere" perspectives? Or if this doesn't happen—if we are indeed fated to always view things partially—are our perspectives all equal in value? Is any one of them as good as the next, or can one be "better," be "more valid"? And again, then, how would we decide this? By what criteria do we make such a determination?

We can see, therefore, that the concept of "perspective" leads directly to such major issues as "reality," "truth" and "knowledge." And with this resonance of implication, this promise of inherent significance, it confirms its promise as a leverage point for my discussion. Enhancing this promise further is the bridge it establishes between "objective" and "subjective": in its very conception, in its structure itself, "perspective" incorporates in a single entity what in our usual view lies distinctly apart; it overcomes from the beginning the stubborn opposition that arises in Realism between two self-standing domains. The stark division between an "objective" and a "subjective" forms for Realism an enduring problem. And by avoiding it, "perspective" removes from its supporting phenomenonological paradigm this major obstacle to systematic cohesiveness.

4

As I proceed, I will first take up the paradigm that

is familiar. Realism is so ingrained in our customary way of viewing things that it will need in some measure to be objectified, to be put at a distance if we are to be able to entertain an alternative. In order to accomplish this, I will attempt to convey a sense of its whole; I will describe both the function it is designed to serve and the assumptive structure that it lays down in order to carry out this function. The former consists in providing explanations for certain fundamental problems of the kind I have already mentioned, in explaining for instance how we come by the contents of our consciousness. By showing how Realism goes about this task and by bringing to light both its successes and its failures, I will hope to be able to convey this comprehensive "sense of the whole."

With this critique as preparation, then, I will begin in my second chapter on the phenomenological alternative. I will turn to the two basic elements of conscious life, the percept and the concept, and examine the way in which each of these is formed. In our customary view, percepts are the concrete material supplied by our perceiving and concepts the more general material that is abstracted from them. My analysis will show, however, that percepts unavoidably contain a factor of *organization*; and since this is the special function of the concept, they must include in their constitution this conceptual element. Such a proposal, however, breaches our customary distinction between what is "concrete" and what is "abstract"; and in order to resolve this, I will advance a theory of the concept that departs radically from our traditional doctrine of abstraction. It is a theory that will place the concept squarely at the center of conscious construction. And in its turn, this step will give us an intimation of the *unity* that runs through this multidirectioned construction.

In my third chapter, I will continue to examine the conceptions that contribute to the needed systemization. I will return to the function of perception and show how, in its early achievement of "constancies," it forms the structure that will serve as the mold for further formations: this is the "transformation group." But in order to grasp perception in its entirety, in order to comprehend it in the full range of its functioning, I will need to bring into view a feature that is prominent in the kind of perceiving that takes place in children and those who live in mythological cultures. This is its emotional side. Perception is intimately connected with our affective life; and in these earlier stages, it is not devoted to putting before us fixed objects so much as conveying emotional valences. It produces here a different kind of experience, one that is directly keyed to the subject's affect. And it is in this unsettled matrix that mythological thinking arises: it is in this affectively-keyed experience, in this shifting and changing milieu, that belief in magic, superstition, and ritual find root.

The question that comes to the fore, then, is how the stable objects that we have in our more advanced experience emerge. In examining this, I am led to the key role in conscious structuring of the symbol. It is by means of *language* that this development takes place;

more particularly, it is through the *name* that we are able to hold and repeatedly return to what is temporary and fleeting. The fundamental role that symbolic action plays in conscious construction thus comes into view. And by attending to the way in which the symbol's two internal moments of "sign" and "signified" vary in their degree of differentiation, I am able to show how the great modes of cultural expression—the worlds of myth and objective "things," of religion and science, of art and mathematics—are formed. It remains only to return to the fundamental problems and demonstrate how in this new system these problems are resolved, then, to complete my exposition of the phenomenological paradigm.

In my final chapter, I will leave these systematic considerations aside and follow the trail of "perspective" in more everyday contexts. It is important to extend our understanding of this concept into our daily life if we are to realize its true scope and significance. To do this, I will examine the role that perspective plays in our development as individuals, in the dialogue that is constitutive of a society, and in the creative process. Finally, I will contextualize the ideas I have been discussing in relation to various trends that are current in present-day philosophy: I will show how philosophy has anticipated in major ways this alternative paradigm.

5

The task I am setting is by no means an easy one. There are good reasons for philosophy's diminishing interest in a systematic phenomenology, and only one of these is the opacity of its better-known proponents—an opacity that derives both from the failure of these proponents to break definitively with Realism and their inability to sufficiently analyze their fundamental "things." Of even greater importance is the instinctive repulsion we feel towards a standpoint that seems to imply ensconcement in a purely private world, imprisonment in a self-enclosed "mind" that is of uncertain link to any reality. Common sense is affronted; an unacceptable solipsism looms. And pressing questions arise as to how we can have any certainty about the things that we see or think, what the role of "reality" is, and how we can come by these things that occupy our consciousness to begin with.

As I address these questions, I will be presenting my discussion in the form of a simple line of argument, one that will hopefully appeal not only to the trained philosopher but to the reader who is not philosophically sophisticated as well. If indeed the fact of "perspective" and the phenomenological paradigm that supports it have important implications for our everyday living—if, as I claim, they can entirely supplant our received Realism—they must have a significance that extends far beyond the sequestered halls of philosophy. It is all the more important, then, to present these ideas in a way that is simple and straightforward. Jargon will be avoided. And while I cannot promise that the conceptualization itself will be immediately graspable—it is virtually by definition, after all, counter-intuitive—I will make every effort to meet literary standards of clarity and coherence. Detracting in some measure from these standards, unfortunately, will be my reliance upon the masculine pronoun: until a usage is developed that is more impartial and even-handed, stylistic considerations must seem to have to trump the awkwardness of the presently available alternatives.

Chapter 1

REALISM

*"The picture which holds traditional philosophy
captive is that of the mind as a great mirror."*
—Rorty, *Philosophy and the Mirror of Nature*

1

We all start in life as naïve realists. That is, we believe that the things we see, the objects we touch, the events that are going on around us, are "real." These things, these objects, these events are simply and plainly "there." In the immediacy of their presence, in the clear evidence they give of their existence, they brook no uncertainty. We come into the standpoint of Realism as though it was inborn: we begin in life as though Realism was our birthright.

It is not long, however, before we are forced to question these initial beliefs. We notice, for instance, that when we close our eyes, all the solid things of this reality disappear. When we sleep, the entire reality itself vanishes. We are no longer able to hold the opinion that we actually *have* the reality, therefore, and instead form the great division between "objective" and "subjective": we differentiate *things* from the *images*, *per-cepts*, and *ideas* we have of these things, and in this way, move into the position of "sophisticated" Realism.

This becomes the position, then, that we will henceforth occupy. In it, the "reality" becomes pushed back, and what is immediately given—what at any moment we actually "have"—is relegated to the subjective.

Further thought shows, then, the *all-inclusiveness* of this subjective. There is *nothing* that we have, *nothing* that is directly given us, that is not of its nature. We may think initially, for instance, that we can contact the reality directly by going up to something and touching it. But upon further consideration, we see that what we actually have is still only the touch-*experience*—the thing itself is not pressing into our awareness, but is being mediated by our particular sensory system as this exists in us and in our species. And not only everything we start from, but everything we thereupon go to—in our conceptualization about this primary material, in the inferences we draw from it—is similarly of this phenomenological kind. An inference to a real object out there that we take to be evoking our percept of it, for instance, is still an inference: what we directly have is an inference-to-an-object, not an object.

Thus we are forced to a portentous and far-reaching conclusion. *We are each and every one enclosed within a phenomenological world. And we have as little chance of reaching out of this world in the direct grasping of something real as we have of stepping outside our own skin.*

This insight comes to realization only slowly. Indeed, it continues to be ignored in our daily life where a constant awareness of our phenomenological condition would only interfere with our ability to act effectively on things. But in the course of history as well, it could come to definitive formulation only after many centuries. This occurred when Husserl, in the early years of the last century, gave expression to the notion of a "phenomenological reduction." And although he used this expression in different ways at different times (Moran 2000, 146 ff.), the central idea was that of a "reduction" of the former putatively real things to their mental representations. Others before him had grappled with the idea of a totally enclosed phenomenological domain, and among them Kant was particularly tenacious in trying to develop the systematic consequences of this enclosure.[2] But Husserl is to be credited with giving this essential realization—this inescapable feature of the human condition—its most succinct and pithy expression.

Whether perceived only dimly or in full clarity, however, this realization is essential for Realism's *systematic* development. For the reduction gives rise to a number of problems, among them the threat of imprisonment in an all-engulfing "subjective." And in order to extract ourselves from these problems, we must erect a structure that will, by establishing certain postulates and drawing from them their implications, provide us with the needed explanations. It was to this task, then, that Realism in its sophisticated form devoted itself; and the outcome was a full-fledged "paradigm," a philosophical system that became the dominant influence in human thinking.

It is important now to define these problems, for only as we succeed in delineating them clearly and completely will we be able to judge how well Realism succeeds. And since they are problems that attend the phenomenological reduction itself—since they arise as soon as we step out of our naïve outlook in realization that the "real" is not immediately given—they necessarily become a task for any philosophical system: any paradigm that aspires to being a comprehensive explanation-of-things must address them and provide for them satisfactory solutions. When I later present the phenomenological alternative, therefore, I will be under obligation to return to them and submit this paradigm as well to their test.

2

The problems appear to be seven in number.

First and foremost, how do we account for the *contents* of our phenomenological world? How do these things I see and these images I have come about? Why is this world filled with these things rather than those, with animals, trees, and people rather than griffins, centaurs, and unicorns?

Second, what accounts for the *immediacy* that certain things in this world have in comparison with others? What gives the objects that appear in my perception the directness and impact that distinguishes them from similar objects that appear in my thoughts or dreams?

Third, how does my *interpersonal agreement* with others come about? If I point to a tree and say to you, "Look, there's a tree," my experience is that ninety-nine times out of a hundred you will look and agree that there is a tree there also. What makes me able, if I and you live in separate phenomenological worlds, to have the experience I frequently have of agreement with you?

Related to this and even more fundamental is the matter of my own *intrapersonal* agreement. I can look at an object, look away, look back again, and "it" is still there. Or with many things, I can come back another day and "they" will still be there. How do these phenomenological consistencies we call the "identity" of things come about?

Fifth, how do I come by my *intersensory correlations?* I can see an object, then walk up to it and touch it. I can hear a sound, then look in its direction and visually locate its source. What explains these correspondences between two or more of my sensory spheres— these "identities," again, in experiences that have proceeded along different sensory paths?

Then there is the problem of *knowledge.* How can I acquire a knowledge? How can I start from and stay with a phenomenological stuff of some kind and yet feel that I am progressively approaching a "truth"? How is science possible, an enterprise that is devoted to "discovering reality" and convincingly shows that it is making progress towards this goal?

Finally, there is the most unnerving problem of all, the threat of a slide into *solipsism.* If I am totally immersed in the subjective, if what I immediately "have" is always and inescapably of this phenomenological kind, what prevents me from having to conclude that I am just occupying a mind world in which all the things I have are merely the figments of my imagination? What prevents *the* world from becoming *my* world, and I alone with it?

3

Realism proceeds, then, by establishing two primary postulates. In the first, it declares that, while the real things are not present to us directly, they nevertheless "exist out there." A reality *lies behind* the directly given data of our mental world. In the second, it asserts that there is some process by which these real things come into the mind. Some kind of *copy function* exists by virtue of which what is out there becomes transformed into mental contents. With these postulates in hand, then, it proceeds with its explanations.

It accounts for the contents of our phenomenological world by simply invoking its postulates. Trees and people inhabit my mind rather than ghosts and griffins because 1) there is a real world out there that has trees and people in it, and 2) this world gains entry to my mind by means of a copy process.

It asserts that the direct sense I have of the immediacy of certain of my phenomenological contents is nothing but a kind of unconscious awareness of what is copy-derived and what is not. The percept I have of a tree as I look outward carries with it this stamp of the copy process while the same tree in a dream or my imagination does not. Eventually, Realists hope, they will be able to identify the neurological correlates of this unconscious awareness and specify the means by which this "sense of the real" is transmitted.

It dispatches with equal ease the problems of interpersonal and intrapersonal agreement. Since both my world and yours or my own at two points in time are copies under the same function of a one and same real world, they must correspond in their elements and articulation. In both cases, we "stand before the same reality."

Similarly with our intersensory correlations. It says that the similarity-of-experience I have when two different sensory paths are involved is due to the fact that these experiences "arise from the same source." They refer, simply, to a one and same event in the real world.

The problem of knowledge, however, runs into difficulties. So far, Realism has been led to tie the reality bonds at the *source* of our phenomenological world: this world arises, it has said, through the reproduction in our perception of what lies outside, and our other mental functions—our thought, our memory, our imagination—follow and depend upon the data perception supplies. In the case of our knowledge, however, it finds that the "real" is attained only after a long and drawn out process. Furthermore, this is a process that *involves and relies upon* these very subsidiary functions! For the realities established by science—entities like "atom," "gravity," and "gene"—regularly involve operations of inference, hypothesization, and deduction; they stand, not at the *beginning* of the activity, but at the *end*. And so, a first hint of a flaw in Realism's paradigm makes its appearance: a puzzle arises as to how these subjective "verbal" procedures can play the role they do in our cognition and knowledge.

Explanatory elegance returns, however, when Realism passes on to the final problem. It banishes solipsism by asserting simply that our phenomenological world is "held fast," so to speak, to the real world. The individual's primary orientation is toward this outer reality and his constant occupation is to sense and come to know it. Any functions that are not real-world oriented—dreaming, for instance, or fantasizing and artistic creation—are "wayward" in nature; they are departures from the copy activity which, if anything, they distort. In support of this naked valuation, Realists appeal to biological theories about the need of organisms to "adapt": organisms must be in continual contact with the reality, they aver, in order to survive.

4

With this, then, Realism completes its explanatory project. And it is a project that, at first sight, has every sign of being successful. With the exception of the difficulty regarding knowledge, its accounting-of-things is at once compelling and economical. In addition, it has given us the purely *emotional* mooring we need in the face of the reduction. For the personal unsettlement that follows in the wake of our phenomenological condition is not to be underestimated; and this unsettlement has now been defused through a rational understanding. It is little wonder, then, if we develop a strong, even irrational attachment to this particular paradigm: it appeals not only on the basis of reason, but of necessity to our very sanity.

Realism's paradigm has developed serious problems, however, and the difficulty regarding knowledge turned out to be a harbinger of other difficulties yet to emerge. But before we go on to see what these are, it is important to note a highly beneficial consequence of its sophisticated position. This is *the freedom this position bestows on us to construe "reality" just as we wish!* For as long as we occupied our naïve position, we were stuck with a reality that had to be taken just as it presented itself; we were chained to whatever offered itself up in our perception. Now, however, this reality has been moved to a purely *formal* status; it has become an element, simply, in an *explanatory system.* And with this, we acquire complete flexibility in how we will interpret it: *we may make of the reality anything we will!*

This flexibility becomes indispensable to the development, then, of both science and philosophy. In science, it gives the investigator the freedom to continually redefine reality as he pursues his goal of creating a comprehensive explanation of the natural universe. He may construe it now as composed of phlogiston and electric fluid, now of ether and little billiard balls, now of quarks and leptons. And in philosophy, it opens a number of explanatory avenues. If the philosopher is primarily interested in explaining our phenomenal contents, he may posit a reality that consists of substantial "things" that correspond in form and number to the things that are given in our perception; if he is oriented more toward explaining such entities as "number," "truth," and "justice," he may construe it as consisting of abstract ideas; if he is impelled to bring everything into the coherence of a unitary system, he may posit some supreme "spirit," "law," or "principle."

Realism spawns, therefore, a number of sub-philosophies. And as monists spring up to argue with pluralists, realists (small r) with idealists, empiricists with rationalists, a dialectic ensues that is as interminable as time itself. This very interminability, however—this inability to make essential progress over time—would seem to indicate the presence in its system of some inherent flaw. And indeed, this suspicion is confirmed: as the full implications of Realism's postulational direction became clear, systemic problems arose that no amount of philosophic deliberation could resolve. The task of fulfilling Realism's project bogged down in never-ending fixes. And to this day, Realism's enterprise remains essentially uncompleted.

I will turn now to two of the more prominent of these problems. One is the schism that develops between what is "empirical" and what is "logical." The other is the difficulty Realism encounters in explaining its "copying."

5

The first problem derives from Realism's inherent bias. In its fundamental form—in the essential structure it lays down prior to any later excursions into, for instance, rationalism or idealism—Realism fastens upon sensation and perception as the channels through which the all-important reality funnels into the mind. Other mental functions are viewed as secondary and derived: "conception" becomes merely the automatic abstraction that occurs when redundant aspects of the sensory material are washed away; "thought" becomes a secondary association of elements that are already given; "memory" becomes simply a fixing of what the senses bring in.

As it continues, however, Realism discovers that such enterprises as logic and mathematics proceed on a different principle. "Truth" for these enterprises is a matter, not of direct sensory evidence, but of *logical necessity*. In contradiction to what it initially posits, criteria shift to what is *purely rational*. Two standards thus rise to hold sway over Realistic thought, and each becomes the pole for a different emphasis. Sensation- and empirical-based doctrines start with the phenomena that seem to be the direct footprint of a reality outside, while rational- and idealistic-based doctrines incline towards this logical standard.

Science, furthermore—the enterprise that is dedicated to finding the exact nature of the real—only exacerbates the problem. Beginning each new investigative endeavor on the assumption that its ultimate criterion will be "appeal to the senses," it becomes more and more drawn to the opposing pole. In the end, it establishes the connections it weaves between cause and effect (or more recently, its probability determinations) on the basis of *necessary deduction*: it turns decisively into the rational-based, logical path.

Thus the great enigma: How can what is arrived at by *a priori reasoning* have *empirical* power and validity? How can what is *necessary, work*? A fundamental fissure develops within Realism's system, a conflict between two conceptions of "Truth." There is a truth of sensory evidence and there is a truth of logical necessity. And in its entrenchment—in its resistance to any kind of resolution—this fissure prevents Realism from achieving its goal of systematic consistency.

Another and equally damaging problem appears, then, with its second assumption. For when Realism lays down its copy postulate—when it asserts the existence of a process by which the reality can become transported into the mind—it devolves upon itself responsibility for spelling out the means by which this transition is accomplished. Just how does the real—whether it consist of substantial objects, ideal forms, or transcendental spirit—become transformed into phenomenal experience? How is this crucial leap effected? From the "eidola" of Democritus to the present-day arcana of neurophysiology, however, every attempt to answer this question has failed. Every explanation is forced to rely in the end on either a "little man in the head" who magically effects the needed leap or an equally magical act, simply, of *transubstantiation*.

We become apprised of the difficulties involved in such an explanation when we try to lead an outside stimulus—that emanating, say, from a tree—into the phenomenal percept of this tree. Following the light waves that proceed from the physical tree to the retina, we find them setting off chemical reactions that generate in turn electrical impulses. These divide among four optic nerves, then, and thus separated, continue on to the primary visual cortex. From here, they disperse even further among different processing centers and association areas, proceeding eventually, perhaps, to motor pathways. *Nowhere in this entire procession, however, is there a place where everything "ends up"; there is no point along their course where the impulses attain some kind of terminal coherence.* Instead, the picture is one of spreading fractionation: the original stimulus becomes so dispersed in both space and time that it is impossible to say at any given moment just where it is.

Out of this manifold, however, we are required to draw the unitary percept of a tree. Complexity is to give rise to simplicity. Continual change in form is to produce form-identity. Ongoing movement is to eventuate in perceived immobility.[3]

And this is only one side, furthermore, of the general problem. When we turn from its empirical to its purely formal aspect, we again run into a barrier. Realism must of necessity enter a logical enterprise. As with any explanatory system, it must, beginning with its starting point—in this case, the physical stimulus— *derive* what it desires—the phenomenal percept. But how can one draw statements regarding phenomenal qualities like "red" and "loud" from statements regarding real-world configurations or energy patterns? How can one by any rational means derive "hot" or "sweet" from neural impulses or chemical exchanges? Any explanation will necessarily incorporate a logical break, a jump to another category that would fatally interrupt it. In the end, this real-to-mental transformation cannot help but seem a miracle: it has been from its inception a priori inconceivable.

6

All these considerations bring us to a point, now, in which we can see where Realism makes its fundamental error. In laying down its explicit postulates, that of an objective reality "outside" and of a copy process that brings this reality into the mind, it relies upon the assumption of a strict separation between what is "objective" and what is "subjective." It construes its task as one of reconciling two opposing domains, two kinds of "being," the one physical/physiological in nature and the other mental. *This assumption, however, contradicts the phenomenological reduction! It ignores the fact that this "objective" is itself phenomenological in nature!* For all these things and events that we attribute to an external reality are ultimately *percepts and concepts* of things and events. All that we think about and that we consider in our thinking to be "objective" is something that we *think*; all that we are looking at that seems in our perception to be unquestionably "out there" is something that we *see*. And the notion of a "pure objective"—of an objective that has no reference to its phenomenological status—is, therefore, entirely empty: it cannot be filled with any intrinsic content.

In advance of its explicit postulations, then—in advance even of its two fundamental assumptions—

Realism takes another, more far-reaching step. *It rei-fies the categories "objective" and "subjective."* It erects two ontological absolutes, and these stand henceforth at the head of its system, holding this system as in an iron vise. With fate-like persistence, "objective" and "subjective" march into every reach this philosophy makes, now, throwing up antitheses to be resolved, polarities to be reconciled, dualisms to be overcome. And as feuding camps spring up to take opposing sides, Realism's entire enterprise degenerates into incessant struggle; all progress becomes stayed in the inter-minable beat of a stagnant dialectic.

Even the *form* of the Realist's activity reflects this primitive polarization. For every surge the Realist makes toward the objective hurls him back into a pure-ly subjective busywork; every grasp he attempts at "reality" plunges him deeper into internal contrivance. In endless Sisyphean labor, he must strive to evolve from within his system a means for overcoming his own assumptive base. And if there is one lesson we can learn from this centuries-long struggle—if there is one piece of treasure we can redeem from this colossal fail-ure—it is that the more we reach in our philosophy for an objective, the more we become thrown back into a *thoroughly subjective self-involvement by this act of reaching itself.*

This lesson provides us with a guide, then, to the way in which we must proceed. Returning to the phe-nomenological reduction, we must dethrone these two categories; we must remove both objective and subjec-tive from their ontological status and bring them back into the phenomenological domain. Assigned to their proper place, then, these categories enable us to see that—far from representing something absolute, far from referring to two realms of "Being" that stand each in sturdy self-subsistence while awaiting our exploration—*they are instruments for the organization of experience.* They function together as a *principle* that, applied to our phenomenal contents, enables us to sort and order these contents. In the new paradigm, the two self-standing domains that in Realism face us in irreconcilable opposition dissolve into a single dimension of judgment; and this dimension, like others that are active in conscious construction, functions to arrange and organize our "things."

We see how, by applying this principle then, we are able to separate the actual *perception* we have of a tree or a star from our *memory* of the same phenomenon. We see how we are able to differentiate *scientific* notions that we create for "atom" and "black hole" from *mythological* notions for self-absorbed gods. We see how we are able to distinguish between things that we actually *experience* and things that we merely *think.* Instead of standing over us in magisterial authority, "objective" and "subjective" enter our phenomenal world, now, and set within it a *functional* division; and depending on the overall organization that we are at the moment effecting, we are free to shift a content from one side of this division to the other. We reinterpret the stick that "objectively" bends when we place it in water as "subjective illusion," for instance, when we establish a higher-order objectivity that is based upon scientific laws of refraction. We reassign the sun that "objectively" moves from horizon to horizon each day to the status of "subjective appearance" when we adopt the more comprehensive outlook that Copernicus provides in his astronomy.

7

We can begin to see the outline, now, of the paradigm that can replace Realism. It is a paradigm in which "being" gives way to "knowing," in which a single-minded focus on the correct reception of what is out there is replaced by a multidirectioned activity of creative formation. For its source, this paradigm goes back to Kant's revolution: turning us away from the *Dingen an sich* of an external reality and reorienting us to the "constitutive preconditions of experience," this revolution brings our focus to the elements that are necessary for experience to "be." And since experience always comes to us in some *form*—since it appears as a "thing" occupying space, as an "event" coming after or before other events, as "singular" or "plural," as tied to other things or events by chains of "cause"—some kind of *formative agent* is implied. We are thus led into the task of defining these agents and understanding the ways in which this form-giving is carried out; and in turn, this leads us to such templates as "space" and "time," "similarity" and "superior-inferior," "number" and "cause."

Accepting in its full import the phenomenological reduction, then, I will begin by stationing myself in that consciousness in which all our awareness of things takes place and all our perceptions, thoughts, and knowledge have their "being." I will, in Husserl's terms, go back—in a renewed sense—"to the things themselves." Immediately, however, the fundamental problems reappear. How in this new view do we come by the contents of this consciousness? What enables us to distinguish among them which are "valid" and which are not? How do we arrive at that consensuality we have with others in our perception of things? Most pressing of all, how do we avoid the solipsism that seems to be such an inevitable consequence of this phenomenological immersion? If our paradigm is to be successful, if it is to attain the goals both of a comprehensive understanding and internal consistency, it must be able to provide satisfactory answers to these questions.

I will begin by examining the two elements that are basic to conscious life, the percept and the concept. The one provides us with that field of "things" that are spread so autonomously before us, and the other opens the path to those "higher" activities we encounter in reasoning and thought. The one provides our conscious life with what is "concrete," and the other with what, in contrast, is "abstract." Unless we know how these two elements can be understood from a thoroughly phenomenological standpoint, we would lack the ground we need for further construction: any paradigm, whether it be Realistic in orientation or phenomenological, must root itself in an understanding of these most fundamental of conscious elements.

Chapter 2

OBJECT AND CONCEPT

*"For the mind, only that can be visible which
has some definite form; but every form of
existence has its source in some peculiar way
of seeing, some intellectual formulation
and intuition of meaning."*
—Cassirer, *Language and Myth*

1

As we view the things that lie before us when we look out upon the world, we cannot help but notice that we are seeing these things from a particular standpoint. They take their form and their "look" from the position we are occupying in space; for if we change this position, they will automatically change in their look. We recognize, as well, that we do not view them exactly as other people do. Since these other people occupy positions that are different from ours, they will see them differently; these things will have for them a different look.

Furthermore, as we look at our object we become aware that we are seeing only one of its sides. We must

33

change our spatial position in order to see another side, its back, or to view it from above or below. We "have" it in only one of its aspects. And there is no way we can escape this contingency. However we position ourselves, we will never be able to bring into our vision the *whole* of the object.

These facts suggest, then, a certain definition of "perspective." It seems to be twofold in nature. It implies on the one hand some position we take from which we view things, and on the other hand the "something" that presents itself as we stand in this position. "Having a perspective," then, involves both these poles. We could say that a mere standpoint without something to bear upon would be "empty" while a something without standpoint to view it from would be "blind."[4]

Thus, in our conscious awareness, the "things" we have before us never stand alone. They reach back always to an implied position. And since these things seem to be "real," we must say that their very *existence* (perceptually speaking) is held in fee to something personal, to something subjective. Unless we decide as we go along that the unalloyed "real" can somehow be grasped directly, we find at this point that this is a "real" that is thoroughly compromised by subjectivity.

2

But of course we quickly overcome this apparent limitation on the "existence" of things! We do this through our notion of the "object." An object, as we conceive it, consists not only of one of the particular aspects that we can have from this or that position—of what is perceptually given—but of the totality of aspects that can arise from *any* position. It is not simply an "appearance" given in the moment and disappearing when it is replaced by another appearance, but a whole *group* of appearances, actual and potential, taken together. We know that an important step in a child's development is becoming able to have objects when, between the ages of one and two, he or she perfects the ability to introduce into the succession of appearances genuine "things" (Piaget 1954)[5]. For the first time, the child becomes able to achieve amidst the unending flow the important qualities of *permanence* and *stability*.

A critical function thus reveals itself here. This is the operation in our perceptual functioning of "indication." In this process of object-forming, the particular aspect that is present at the moment comes to indicate the other aspects. It is by means of indication that we are able to reach outside the appearance of the moment and point to something beyond; it is through indication that we are able to bring these other sides into the present moment and, putting them in conjunction with what is given, create an "object." Indication thus enables us to "fill" what is actual with the possible; it makes what is given "burgeon" with the not-given.

We are compelled to realize, then, that these objects are not actually "in" our experience! They are not something that we actually at the moment "have"! What we have is only the immediate appearance; it is a "presentation," merely, that passes and is replaced. Since so much of what constitutes these objects is not in an experiential sense "real," then, it must be "ideal"! These objects occupy in fact an ideal space: they inhabit a further realm that we have created and that we are populating now with these "things." It is a space whose occupants possess the virtue that they stand apart from the ceaseless flux of coming-to-be and van-ishing-away: transcending the constant flow of ever-changing appearances, *they lift us out of the immediate.*

And they are things, furthermore, that we may return to again and again! By means of another opera-tion, that of "recognition," we are able to bring into the present something from this realm that has gone by. We are able to recover a previous object on the basis that it seems to us to be "the same" as the one we are now indicating. In another way, then, we are able to bring what is not actual into conjunction with the actual: we are able, by "recognizing" something that is before us and real, to unite it with what at the moment is not real. We are again able to step—this time in a *temporal* sense—into the ideal.

3

Indication and recognition become two essential functions, then, in the building of our perceptual world. But now something important seems to have happened. With this ideal space and these objects, we seem to have overcome the fact of perspective! We seem to have shed our former one-sidedness and freed ourselves from our subjective mooring. And this has occurred in both a spatial and a temporal sense; in regard to both these dimensions, we have been released from the necessity of being bound, always, to some specific position. Though still tied to what is happening in the moment, to what presents itself in the form of an appearance, we have become able to transcend this moment: we have, in significant measure at least, *freed* ourselves from the moment's contingencies.

And the method we have used for accomplishing this has been to take resort to the ideal. Our experience itself, however, seems to contradict such a conclusion. For in our everyday living, we do not consider these objects to be ideal—rather, they seem to us to be unquestionably real. These "stones," "trees," "people" that we are now saying that we see seem in their brazen "thereness" to *lie on a plane* with the appearances. Upon closer examination, however, we realize the error of this presumption: for we live always and only among our appearances. It is that we are looking *through* these appearances, now, to something beyond; instead of being content with the simple immediate, we are using the functions of indication and recognition to transport ourselves from this immediate into our ideal space.[6]

There is a telling sign of this action, furthermore, in the immediate itself. This lies in changes that come over these appearances. For as we engage in this activity of looking through, we are no longer viewing an appearance in the fullness of its presence; we are no longer regarding it as it comes along simply in its unique and colorful "being." Rather, it has taken on the character now of an "aspect" or "side" of something else. It has acquired a quality of "vectorizing," of leading our vision beyond. Thus a newly *functional* element has entered our perceptual world: this world has become infiltrated with an activity of "representation"; and its contents—instead of standing before us in the starkness of their immediacy—are becoming capable of *standing for* and *representing* something else.

And with this, we are acquiring an important new potential. We are becoming able to *dominate* our environment. Instead of being the passive captives of what is happening around—instead of being the prisoners of whatever pulls our attention at the moment—we are thrusting ourselves into the flow and exerting on it a power of active formation. We are opening a path to *control* over what happens around; and as time goes on, we will be pursuing this path with greater and greater determination.

4

Now an important polarity begins to form. This is the division between a "subjective" and an "objective." For with this separation of what is transient from what is permanent, we are led to differentiate two great realms. The one contains everything that is strictly immediate, that is temporary and passing; and the other contains everything that is lasting, that prevails through different spatial and temporal changes. The one takes the character of the unpredictable and—in a way—fickle; and the other takes the character of the enduring and stable. In our experience, therefore, a kind of inner division takes place: what is transitory is set off against what is steadfast; what is subjectively dependent opposes itself to what stands in august self-sufficiency.

With this, moreover, grounds are created for a new kind of "reality." For the contents of this objective realm seem to be more real than the passing appearances. In their dependable thereness and continuity over time, they possess a substantiality that our appearances lack. Two criteria for the real thus form, one of simple "immediacy" and one of "objectivity." On the one hand, the appearances that flow before us in our immediate experience are still of the nature of a *fundamentum*: they provide us with the basic material on which anything further is built. On the other hand, the contents of this "objective" transcend the changeability of this material: they possess the reality of the self-confidently enduring. And so we come into possession of two different kinds of "real"; and of the two, it is the latter that seems to present us with what is *really* real.

We enhance this construal further, then, in two important ways. First, we augment our impression of the solidity of the objective by bringing into play our sensory mode of touch. We coordinate with our object-indicating appearances the tactual sensations we have when we go up to something we see or hear and touch it. In this way, we provide our objects with a quality of "concreteness" that separates them further from the ephemerality of appearances. We introduce into our experience the important feature of "tangibility."

Second, we open an avenue with this objective realm into intersubjectivity. For we consider its objects to be capable of being seen, felt, and recognized by others. And making attempt then to communicate with these others, we enter with them into a task of mutual determination. We engage with them in an activity of articulating, naming, and describing. In pursuing this task, we utilize the medium of *language*: it is by means of our linguistic forms that we are able to carry this activity out and achieve the all-important quality of *consensual* validation for what is "there."

As the meaning of objectivity fills and enriches in this way, then, we come more and more to view ourselves as standing before a great domain of "Objective Being." It is a domain that is boundless in its extent and that holds promise in its inherent mystery of exciting discovery. Seeking to actualize this potential, therefore, we begin on an enterprise of exploration; we attempt to ascertain the nature and qualities of its occupants. As before, however, this "exploration" will consist of *originative construction*: it will be effected through the engenderment of new and innovative "things." And bringing us in this way into an important new estate, it will produce a special fruit of our step into the ideal: *it will make of our objective realm a doorway into "knowledge."*

5

We set forth on this enterprise by inquiring into the relationships that exist among these objects. And continuing with our ideal construction, we create new templates, then, for the forms these relationships may take. Along one avenue, we devise templates for ordering our objects in "space" and "time." The former enables us to put one object next to, behind, or in front of another. The latter, introducing a dimension of past-present-future, enables us to consider one object as earlier than, contemporaneous with, or later than another.

In another direction, we begin to establish determinate groupings. We utilize a principle of "similarity" to establish a template for "class," relating together by means of a class of "dog," for instance, certain four-footed objects as these appear at different times and in different places, and by means of a class of "tree" certain tall, leafy objects as these in turn appear. Turning to these classes themselves, then, we form further classes that are subordinate and superordinate to these: we relate together through a class of "terrier" dogs that manifest in their presentation certain specific characteristics; and by means of another class of "animal," we create an umbrella that brings together with our dogs "giraffes," "deer," and "mice."

As we proceed in this way, we become able to reach across greater and greater distances in our experience. We become able to connect our varied appearances more powerfully than we could with our simple "indication" and "recognition." These steps cannot be taken, however, without bringing about an important change in experience itself: for as our appearances lead us more and more into the larger spatial, temporal, class complexes we have constructed, they become read as "instances," merely, of something else. They become emptied even further of their unique and individual character. Experience as a whole, therefore, *fades*; it diminishes in its color and richness. In the process of elaborating our objective domain, we have traded in the freshness of the living present for the paleness of the always-there; we have exchanged the excitement that accompanies the ever-changing for a dull predictability. Leaving behind the ever-fresh world of the child, we have stepped into the quite ordinary world of the adult.

Another important template awaits definition, however, and this extends our organizational reach even further. Having leaned thus far in our relating of things on the principle of "similarity"—having established through our classes the ability to see what is never-endingly different as in one or another way "the same"—we have remained tied for the most part to the mere appearance-of-things. Indeed, we have been able in such higher classes as "vehicle" and "building" to transcend to a degree this limitation: by changing the basis on which we relate things from *form* to *function*, we have been able to tie together experiences that, appearance-wise, have very little similarity. Now, however, we break with the necessity for similarity entirely: by constructing objects that *stand behind* others, we create "sources" from which these others may be derived. We introduce the entirely fresh template of *cause*. And relating things now to these deeper sources, we are able to bring to conscious life an important new dimension: we are able to introduce into its organizing the power of *"explanation."*

Thus, by positing an object called "gravity" and explaining with it the uniform characteristic that physical bodies exhibit of falling, we are able to draw together the entire universe of natural event. By positing an object called "libidc" and explaining with it various psychological features, we are able to create a source that stands within the array of human personalities. Our previous "phenotypical" objects have become supplemented now with deeper "genotypical" objects. Objects that have been oriented towards surface similarities in our direct experience-of-things have been supplemented by objects that function to "explain" what happens in this experience. And though still farther now from what we directly experience, these new objects have immeasurably enhanced our ability to bring together what in this experience is scattered and diverse.

6

More and more, then, the overriding goal that pulls us through all our conscious construction emerges clearly to view. This is to *bring to our experience an inherent unity*. It is to make of the endless succession of appearances—of the disorganized diversity that moment to moment assaults us—*an ordered whole*. Our means for doing this has been to step away from the immediate and enter an ideal world in which the elements of this world increase in their "generality." And in measure as we have done this, we have acquired—in both its senses—"comprehension": we have increased the quantity of material that we are able at any given moment to hold in our grasp; and at the same time, we have come to better and better *understand* what the present moment brings.

The objects of this world are all, furthermore, *relational* in nature! Whatever their level of generality, they consist of *vehicles for the relating of other things together!* As we have gone on, then, our ideal world— this objective domain—has begun to resemble a great tapestry that is woven of these different threads of relationship. Each element in this tapestry has become more and more "contexted"; by virtue of its placement over and over and in different ways in these forms of "time," "class membership," "cause," etc., its position within the whole has become more determined. And so we have become able, by riding on these relationship-lines of "behind" and "in front of," "before" and "after," "the same as" and "causing," to travel from one object to another. We have acquired the ability to *transport ourselves* from any point in this tapestry to any other. To the extent that our object space has become a well-knitted whole, therefore, any single element in it has come to "imply" the others; and our constructed world—our ideal world of objectivity—has come to resemble, in a rough way, a mathematical system.

7

But now, we have to turn to a question that may well have been a troubling one in the course of my discussion. This is the way in which I have been using the term "object." For in encompassing with this term virtually everything we have, in including such diverse things as "tree," "vehicle," and "gravity," I seem to have strayed more and more from our common understanding of what an object *is*. Aren't many of the examples I have been giving in actual fact *concepts*? Do we not in common parlance speak of the *concept* of "tree," the *concept* of "vehicle," the *concept* of "gravity"? And as concepts, mustn't they then be "abstractions" from more primary contents, the representations of what these contents hold in themselves that is general? In my discussion, I have made no reference to either abstraction or generalization! I have pointed instead to such entirely different operations as "indicating" and "organizing."

And these operations, I have shown, reach down to even our most basic objects! Even those concrete things that supposedly compose the material from which our concepts are drawn—the *individual* terrier, oak, person that we encounter in our direct experience—have been shown to be their products! In this case, we will remember, these operations were carried out with respect to appearances: they consisted in the basic activities of "indicating" and "recognizing." Where, then, is the "simple material" from which our concepts are to be drawn? What in this accounting provides the *fundamentum* that is needed for this putative march into the abstract? At every level, it seems, we encounter only this activity of organization: our objects have again and again dissolved in their very "being" into relational complexes.

Clearly, then, there is a need here for clarification. And in order to provide this, I will propose that we consider all our objects, now, to be *concepts*. I will suggest that this universal function of organization that we are everywhere encountering is, properly understood, a *conceptual* function. From this standpoint, then, we would say that the diversity that we have been finding among our objects is simply a reflection of the different ways in which this conceptual activity is carried out: it is, in short, a *functional* diversity. And we would understand that what we have been led back to in examining this functional diversity is nothing but the primary avenues we form for relationship in general: as "templates" we have constructed for space and time, similarity and difference, hierarchy and cause, they are the general *forms* that relationships take.[7]

This proposal, however, flies even more in the face of our common understanding! For how do we reconcile what seems—at one of its levels at least—to be unquestionably *substantive* with this purely ideational notion of a "concept"? How can all these entities that impress us as solid "things"—that we encounter in our experience as a concrete dog, tree, etc.—be said to be nothing but a tissue of relations? Surely I have carried my idealism too far! I have jeopardized my entire analysis by failing to recognize a distinction that is obvious to even the most unsophisticated observer, the difference between what is *concrete* and what is *abstract*.

The only way out of this puzzle is to probe more deeply into the nature of the concept. And in particular, it is to bring under scrutiny the time-honored notion of "abstraction." This notion is a veritable pillar of Realism's system: by declaring that what is more general is a distillation of what reality directly gives us in the form of the concrete, it reinforces the fundamental dependence of this system on an authoritative "outside." It pushes perception into primacy among our mental functions and makes of concepts and the rational operations that stem from them mere derivatives. This doctrine must be challenged, then, if I am to continue on my phenomenological path: I must find some other principle on which to base the concept if I am to remain consistent with my phenomenological principles.

8

Replacing the primacy of the percept with the primacy of the concept cannot help but radically change our ordinary understanding of what a concept is. In our customary view, a concept is the pale residue that is left when percepts that have some property in common are gathered together and their differences washed away. It is an "essence" that, lying unknowingly amidst our perceptions, awaits the stripping away of what is extraneous in these perceptions—what is variable and contingent—to become visible. In forming concepts for "tree" and "house," for instance, I simply ignore all the distracting qualities that the individual trees and houses that I have encountered in my experience have. And so, concept-forming in this view is a relatively passive process: the injection into it of anything that was creative would inevitably spoil it; any hint of something that was genuinely new would irretrievably corrupt it.

From the time of its inception with Aristotle, however, this doctrine has encountered difficulties. The most obvious of these is that we cannot always *find* the experiences from which such concepts are putatively drawn. How can we arrive at such abstractions, for instance, as "quarks," "electrons," and "unicorns"? How can we have a concept for a number like 6234? What concrete perceptions form the basis of our notions for a "nondimensional point" or "non-Euclidean space"? How can we have abstractions for numbers that are even *defined* as "imaginary" or "irrational"?

A second problem concerns the question of how something that is so second-order and effete can exercise the force it does in our thought. In science, the enterprise that most vigorously seeks concepts that will be productive, the procedure runs directly counter to the one that Realism postulates. For science never advances simply from particulars to universals; it does not, in a progression from concrete "things" to abstract species and genera and then on to such all-encompassing notions as "being," *lose* the particular in some vast generic emptiness. On the contrary, it strives to ever more sharply *define* the particular; it attempts to *determine* individual things in their nature and functioning. Thus science pursues an entirely different path: when it instills order into such particulars as chemical elements, astronomical observations, and biochemical facts through concepts like "atom," "quark," and "gene," it provides these particulars with a determinate position within a larger whole; and it is this position, with all its wealth of relational implication, that defines for science their inherent "nature."

But quite beyond these objections, the most damaging problem is the vicious circle into which this doctrine falls. For what makes us able to draw together *just these particular perceptions*, the perceptions that give rise to the concept? What operating principle enables us to say of one as it comes along that it "belongs" and of another that it doesn't? We must already be applying some rule of selection! And for all intents and purposes, *this rule must be the very concept that is being "derived"!* The explanation thus devolves into a *petitio principii*: it assumes the very thing that it sets out to explain.

9

Clearly, another theory of the concept is required, one that accords better with its actual usage. And we find this when we replace a substantial approach—an approach that views the concept as a pale and weakened essence of something more "material," of full-blooded percepts—by a functional approach, an approach that focuses on what the concept does. In this new formulation, we define the concept as *a rule by means of which things are related* (Cassirer 1923, 16 ff). Both these elements, the "rule" and the "things," can be represented, then, in an expression of the form

$$f(a, b, c, \ldots)$$

where "f" denotes a rule of some kind that is being applied, and "a, b, c, …" the elements that this rule is ordering. The concept "tree," for instance, expresses a

rule by means of which an unlimited number of individual experiences—read, now, as instances of "tree"—
may be brought into conjunction with each other. The
concept "house" posits a rule that will coordinate as
individual a's, b's, and c's the individual houses I
encounter in my experience.

Two moments are thus defined, the one representing the concept's "intensional" aspect and the other its
"extensional" aspect. And we need only run the variations that are possible on these two moments to arrive
at the various features that the concept exhibits.

Its distinctive "generality," for instance, derives
from the fact that there is no restriction, on the one
hand, as to the nature of these a's, b's, and c's. They
may be "real" things or concepts-of-things, numbers
or geometric forms, other series or series of series.
Nor is there any restriction, on the other hand, as to
the principle that is being applied. This may be a rule
of "similarity" such as enables us to form our classes, a
rule of "superordinate-subordinate" that enables us to
produce a botanical table of species and genera, a rule
of "side by side" that generates the order of coexis-
tence we call "space," of "after each other" that generates the order of succession we call "time," of "condi-
tional upon" that generates the order of dependency
we call "cause."

Secondly, a concept's elements are no longer lost
in generic emptiness, now, but preserved in their individual "being." In this new formula, explicit denota-
tion is given to these a's, b's, and c's; and this makes it
possible to identify the kind and degree of their inter-

connection. We may define for them a relation of "symmetry," for instance, in which whatever relationship holds between the first and the second also holds between the second and the first. We may define a relation of "transitivity" in which, if the first has a certain relation to the second and this second to a third, the first will also have this relation to the third. We may define a "progressive" series in which, once the first member is established, the rule of organization will determine what each succeeding member will be. In comparison with the concept-structures formed by mathematics, we find, our everyday concepts are relatively "loose": they instill only a minimal degree of cohesiveness among their elements, and these elements occupy their field in no particular order.

Most important of all, however, is the purchase this conception gives us now on the process by which "knowledge" is attained. For it is clear from this formula that the concept has unlimited potential for enrichment. In a process of continual complexifying, we may enter into a new concept as fresh a's, b's, and c's concepts that have already been formed. Thus we may take concepts we have defined for individual plant types and, by specifying some anatomical or functional feature as our principle of ordering, organize these into a second-level concept for "species"; and by searching then for the more powerful principle that will bring our different species into coordination, we may generate the still higher-order concept-form of "genus." Or we may take geometrical elements that are entirely different in form such as points, lines, circles, ellipses, parabolas, and hyperbolas, and by finding a principle that succeeds in drawing them into a group (embodied algebraically in this case in the second degree equation), create of this diversity an organized unity.

At each of these steps we gain a greater *power of survey* over the particulars. We achieve a wider and more comprehensive *knowledge*. By gathering together perspectives that have hitherto been separate into more comprehensive perspectives, therefore, we are able to create more potent standpoints from which to view things. And by stamping these new perspectives with a special word, expression, or formula, we provide them with the handles by which they may be entered into still further series: we achieve with them still more encompassing perspectives.[8]

And so we find the notion of "perspective" re-entering our discussion! Indeed, we have never escaped it. For much as our most basic objects seemed to free us from the burden of one-sidedness—much as they seemed to release us from the need for never-ending perspective-taking—they only established *at a higher level* this very same contingency; they moved perspective-taking to a different plane where it operated in a broader, more universal way. For each such object now represented some kind of "take" on experience. Whether it was created at the concrete level of the "thing" or further on in conceptual development— whether it was the individual dog we were viewing at the moment or the "dog" or "animal" we were contemplating in our thought—it posited some *standpoint* from which to view experience as a whole. Thus the essential structure that we defined earlier was still in operation: we were as firmly locked into "perspective" as we had been with our appearances.

10

This shift in the focus of our conceptualization from "object" to "concept" brings to singular clarity, now, the *power of formation* that rules conscious construction. As we accustom ourselves to this new view and learn to follow the concept's coordinative reach into our diverse perceptual and conceptual material, we see thought breaking free of its long bondage to the sensory and stepping forth in exercise of its inherent potential. What was passive from the standpoint of the abstractive view now becomes active; what was the constriction of a material interpretation becomes the flexibility of a functional one. And so thought, no longer confined to reshaping merely what the senses bring in, cuts its ties to the terrestrial and lifts, then soars to ever wider horizons of universality. Like the lightning that jabbed into the primordial atmosphere creating new forms and life, our concepts strike again and again into the dark substance of experience, crystallizing therein fresh chains of "being" and illuminating in ever-new ways the material we already have.

And with this, we are able to come to a new understanding of the way in which an object acquires its "thingness." The qualities of independence and objectivity that characterize the object are a direct consequence, we see, of this conceptual act of *rule-stamping*.

Whenever a group of particulars—appearances, first-level objects, concepts—takes on some order through the imposition of a rule, a new *singularity* is created; a one thing stands before us where previously there had been many. It is by this means, then, that the "thing" acquires its authority: standing as something constant amidst the change, it becomes read now as self-sufficient; and these acts, repeated over and over, gradually build that "objective" domain that stands sturdily in defiance of the turbulence of the given.

This entire process has as its outcome, then, *understanding*. Whenever we come to newly "understand" something, we are signaling our achievement of some kind of order amidst the confused. We are indicating our establishment of a "one in the many." In describing the experience we have at these times, we use the term "insight": we have been gifted, we say, with sudden insight; we have been graced—as though, often, from outside—with illumination. When a one appears where before there had been many—when a new "being" all at once takes form in the midst of what had hitherto been dispersed—we have been endowed, it seems, with revelation. And we name the mysterious process by which this has occurred "discovery."

11

My discussion brings us to the point, now, that we see the need for a more comprehensive frame into which the different ideas I have been advancing may be placed. Among other things, this frame would accord recognition to the universality of perspective; it would posit the centrality in mental life of form-making; it would honor the human capacity for creativity. In all these respects, Realism fails. Oriented as it is toward an outer reality, it forces us to try to make our mental contents accurately reflect this reality; perspectives, therefore—yielding only partial and subjective accountings of things—are something to be overcome. Consumed with effecting everywhere an *adequatio rei et intellectus*, it ignores our constructive form-making; we are to march in Lockestep from passively received products of the senses to abstraction of their essences and cannot let itself be sidetracked, therefore, by the merely "imaginative." Concerned always about "reflecting," it finds creativity inscrutable; the originality that is everywhere apparent in myth, in art, in literature, in science, is simply inexplicable.

What is needed, then, is no less than an encompassing new perspective. Like all perspectives, this would impose a changed valuing-of-things. It would bring elements that were subordinate in Realism's perspective to the fore and push others that had been important into the background. But its primary feature would be that, in rejecting recourse to an external reality, it would be *phenomenological* in orientation; it would replace dependency on what was foreignly "outside" with a dignifying of experience.

And so my next step will be to describe essential features of this paradigm. In doing this, I will be under obligation to face two essential tests. I will need to show that the formulations this paradigm yields are truer to our actual experience-of-things than

Realism's. And I will need to resolve satisfactorily the fundamental problems.

Chapter 3

THE PHENOMENOLOGICAL PARADIGM

*"All culture takes place in and proves itself
in the creative process, in the activity of the
symbolic forms, and through these forms life
awakens to self-conscious life, and becomes mind.*
—Cassirer, *The Philosophy of Symbolic Forms*

1

The steps I have taken thus far have made us aware of the presence in our conscious functioning of ideality. We have seen this in the dissolving of our solid "things" into purely relational syntheses, into complexes in which what was directly before us was combined with experiences that were merely possible; in the replacement of a materially oriented "abstractive" theory of the concept by a theory that was purely functional; and in general, in the dissolution of "being" into series of determinate conceptual chains. If we were to identify the distinguishing features of the new paradigm in comparison with Realism, one of these would certainly be this ideality. And we must try to understand it systematically, now, in terms of its place in an overall system.[9]

But Realism itself has already taken a step in this direction! As it advanced into its sophisticated form, we saw, it loosened the tight grip of "reality," the mesmerizing thrall that the things around us exert. It pushed this reality back to the position of *assumption*, merely, rather than something that was given; it transformed it from plain and certain "fact" to tantalizing riddle, to theatre upon whose stage we were free to project whatever play and actors we needed to effect our understanding. Indeed, this loosening was achieved only in part; the reality hovered "out there," now, pressing in on us with irresistible force as it produced our perceptions, and through them, our entire mental edifice. But in principle, the far-reaching division between "reality" and "mind" had been achieved; and the way was opened to the great systems of philosophy and science that would proceed to create, now, this play and these actors.

The step that Realism took remained, indeed, continually in jeopardy. Again and again in the long history of their paradigm, Realists succumbed to the temptation to collapse this division and merge the mental back again with the real. This showed itself not only in our common sense outlook where our practical engagement with the things around us virtually mandated that we ignore our phenomenological condition, but at higher explanatory levels as well. At these levels, we find rationality being deserted for the mystical, for instance, when resort is taken to the "spiritual" or "transcendental": postulation is made of such special capacities as "intuition" and "Nous" that, by enabling us to attain oneness with the universe at large, provide a kind of direct and unmediated knowing. One can gain knowledge, it is claimed, by simply fusing consciousness with the very Being itself. In another direction, the mental is simply reduced to the physical. Any qualities that are unique to the mind are denied, and such phenomena as thoughts, images, and memories are interpreted as events that are purely neurophysiological in nature: they are emanations, simply, of the brain (cf. Dennett 1991).

But if effacing the distinction between reality and the mind—if undoing this philosophic accomplishment that had only with difficulty been won—proves in every case to be futile, only one direction remains. This is to continue with the divorce that Realism has begun and challenge even further the place that an "outside" has in our systematic understanding. It is to continue on this path of separation and see if we can arrive at a truer understanding of this reality-mind relationship, an understanding that neither regresses into a mystical union of the two nor devalues the special qualities of mind.

A good place to begin on this endeavor is in the domain of perception. Nowhere does Realism sink its foundations more deeply than in the belief that it is in *perception* that things are presented most nearly "as they are." And much as my previous analysis has cast doubt on this belief by showing the inevitable presence in perception of what is not immediate, of what is

ideal, I will need to return to it now for further examination: I will need to still more irrevocably shake
loose the perceptual object in its stark facticity.

2

I begin by calling attention to the fact that perceptual objects appear the way they do because of our personal interests and attitudes. If, say, a house painter, an
architect, and a builder are walking down a street
together, they are likely to perceive the houses that are
on the sides of this street in different ways. The
painter will notice their exterior surfaces, the condition of their paint, their occasionally unusual color.
The architect will be drawn to their overall style, the
presence among them of any architectural originality,
the exemplification of this or that historical period.
The builder will see features that have to do with
solidity and general construction—a rotting foundation here, loose clapboards there, a deteriorating
chimney will be what press themselves into his awareness. Each will see these houses in accord with his own
interests; and if asked afterwards to make a representation of what they have seen, they will likely produce
very different drawings.

Similarly, a child and an adult on a walk together
will perceive a dog they encounter in very different
ways. The adult sees simply "a dog," a member of a
general category-of-object. She may take note of its
particular breed and any unusual characteristics it has.
The child on the other hand will see the animal in
more sensory-emotional fullness. Less given to cate-

gorizing her experience and more on a level with the animal in size, she will see something that "comes on" to her with particular intensity. It appears to her as a ball of black furry action with *teeth*.

Such examples may be multiplied indefinitely, and investigation of the perceptual experience of children, indigenous peoples, and disturbed individuals has been endlessly instructive in its illustration of the different kinds of world that people inhabit. The lesson to be drawn from these observations is that we each *make* this world, in part at least, in accord with inherent biases: our previous experience, our present interests and intents, our age, our ingrained attitudes—all shape what, for us, is "there." And if we assume that others are seeing things just as we do, we are likely to be simply indulging our innate egocentricity: we are perpetuating the belief we held as a child that we all look out upon the *one* world, and that we must see things, accordingly, in just the same way.[10]

These considerations seem to bring us uncomfortably close to a solipsism, however, and the Realist moves back to another position. While the things we see are indeed subject to these injections of personal bias, he now says, they still contain a *hard objective core*. They possess within these purely subjective elaborations an *irreducible perceptual kernel*. This is what remains constant through all these personal vagaries; this is what gives a faithful reflection of the reality outside. Going on with our examination, then, we attempt to locate this perceptual core: we try to make contact with and bring to exposure this fundamental objective component.

We take for analysis the chair that is in front of us and narrow our attention to its purely sensory qualities. Already, however, we see that we have introduced into our experience an element of subjectivity! For in perceiving this object as a "chair," we have implicitly judged it as *belonging* to this category; we have judged that it is not, for instance, a "stool," a "seat," or a "box." Similarly with other things—if we perceive a "house," we have judged it not to be a "shed," a "cabin," or a "garage"; if we perceive a "tree," we have judged it not to be a "shrub," a "bush," or a "pole." Every time we see something *as* something, we have judged it *into* this category—and correspondingly out of other categories that lie more or less close to it in form or function. Anything can become what it is only by emerging from a virtual surround formed of the various categories-of-things that it might be. And again, we are forced to conclude that what is ideal—in this case, what constitutes this virtual surround—is inescapably present in what is experientially "given."

Our chair, however, still possesses a certain core content, and it can be argued that this active categorization, subjective though it may be, does not touch this content. Above and beyond any such conceptual endowment, the Realist will say, it presents a purely *visual* character. It has a certain form, a certain size, a certain color, an appearance of solidity. It is to these qualities, then, that we re-orient ourselves. Attempting once more to expunge from our experience any kind of mentalistic contribution, we immerse ourselves now in our chair's purely *material* presence. We attend to its character as the simple sense-product it is being claimed to be.

We take first its form, its visual "look." As we have seen, however, this form is not the *whole* of the chair. Other, quite different forms will appear as we walk around and look under and over it. All these "sides," furthermore, are essential to my perception! For what I see is not simply a two-dimensional construction; it does not appear to me as a cardboard cutout that has been cleverly designed to present just the aspect that is now standing before me. It appears in its very look, rather, to be *solid!* It is an *"object"!* And so we are reminded once again that, in this important characteristic of form, we are making use of the ideal: we are projecting into and behind what is actually being given the possibility of other visual forms that are not being given.

We go on, however, to consider its color. Our chair is brown. But wait! Is it not actually red? In seeing it as brown, are we not adjusting for the fact that we are viewing it in the light of the setting sun? As any artist will be quick to point out, a chair that appears to be brown is actually red at sunset, black at dusk, and green in a room illuminated through green-tinted windows. How can we say, then, that we are responding to the purely perceptual? How can we avoid concluding again that what we see as the object's "actual" color is arrived at only after a complex process of interpretation that takes into account the ambient illumination in which this object stands?

We continue on nevertheless and turn our attention to our object's size. It stands before us at a certain relative height; it has a certain relative width. These "relatives," however, trip our suspicion. They remind us of demonstrations that have totally deceived us in this matter of size. For if we look through a keyhole into a specially constructed room in which all the furniture is reduced to half its usual size, we soon see a chair in this room as completely "normal." Its apparent size shows itself to be a function of the visual context in which it is being viewed. Again, then, the "actual" has melted into a complex of conditions: what we directly see shows itself to depend on factors other than what is immediately given.[11]

We persist, however, and consider the last of these perceptual properties, our object's appearance of solidity. The chair we are viewing looks "heavy." It conveys a sense of concrete substantiality. How can we know this about it, however, without actually going up to and hefting it? How can we know from our position at a distance that it is not an artfully constructed balloon ready to go up the moment we touch it? We say that certain cues inform us as to this characteristic, that we are responding to subtle qualities such as its texture and the way internal shadows are cast upon its surface. But again, then, we are *inferring* this quality of solidity: rather than simply taking up into our awareness what is given, we are engaging in a complex process of mental interpretation!

In sum, then, we have failed to produce evidence for the kind of direct perceptual reception that Realism is claiming. Any straightforward "copying" has escaped us; and what has been revealed instead has been the presence everywhere of acts of judgment, inference, and mental interpretation. The objects that are given us in our perception *always* contain, apparently, more than meets the eye; they *always* burgeon, as something "actual," with the "virtual."

It has been impossible, furthermore, to separate these two factors! Our chair actually *appeared* as three-dimensional rather than plane. It actually *looked* brown rather than red. The judgments, inferences, and interpretations we were making entered as very ingredients of the objects themselves. They weaved themselves inextricably into what we perceived as "there."

Thus, we seem to see emerging here a special kind of relationship, an intimate *conditioning* of something by something else. We will return to this relationship later. But meantime, Realism finds itself in its classic quandary. How can something that is *physical* in origin be combined with something that is *mental*? How can we understand the integration of these two factors that are so different in their origin and character? Perception is to be the straightforward transmitting of what is out there into the mind; it is to represent the place where reality and mind meet. How are we to understand this infecting of what should be purely *physiological*, then, with judgments, inferences, and interpretations that stem from the mind?[12]

It might occur to us at this point that a reversal of what the Realist proposes would have better success. If instead of conceiving perception as the *precursor* of our mental processes we conceive it as the *product* of these processes, we would be able to replace the division that

Realism falls into with a single unitary source. And if we could, on the basis of such a position, plumb our perceptual experience to its very depths—if we could so completely parse our perceptual objects that no residue remained—we would have laid the groundwork for a uniform explanation; a continuous path would stretch from the most concrete of conscious levels to the most abstract.

We are not ready to pursue this avenue, however, for Realism has not yet exhausted its argument. By making a small but significant conceptual change—by shifting the weight of its argument from *perception* to *sensation*—it is able to preserve its essential thesis. It makes the assertion now that, in order to find this transition from reality into the mind, we must go to a still more primitive level of perceptual functioning: we must seek it, not in our perceptual "objects," but in *raw sensation*. It will be at this near-physiological level that the necessary copying takes place; it will be in the untouched "sensation" that we will come upon our quarry. Let us turn to this proposal, then, and see if this time we can find a process in which no trace of the mental can be found.

3

In order to avoid the subjective form-giving that all too inevitably clings to our perception of entire objects, we are forced to leave the more meaningful contexts in which these objects arise and bring our focus to mere part-experiences. We must, in short, regress our experience to the simplest and most primitive level possible. Fortunately, special reduction techniques have been developed to help with this undertaking. By rolling a sheet of paper and looking at something through it, for instance, we are able to avoid any conscious awareness of a "thing." What we see is simply a plane surface—a portion, say, of a table top—that seems entirely lacking in any meaningful shaping.

Applying this procedure, then, we are first struck by the formlessness of what we see. A mere "content" appears, something that seems devoid of all shape or determination. As we continue to look, however, our initial impression changes. Certain features emerge, certain attributes such as shadings of lighter and darker, a texture, a particular color. Our content shows at least the rudiments of quality; it possesses a definite and distinctive "character."

And this character must, again, indicate our form-making activity! For these shadings can come to our awareness only by virtue of implicit judgments we make as to what is "same" and what is "different": only on the basis of such judgments can *differences* appear, can one part of the surface be set off from and contrasted with another. The hue it possesses, in turn, requires the evocation of our internalized color spectrum: for it is only by referring our content to the entire range of colors and by giving it a determinate position within this range that we can endow it with its identity of, say, light brown.

Furthermore, elements of this content very likely look familiar. They seem to be similar to other content-experiences we have had. There must be, then, an active engagement of our memory, an intrusion into the sensory process from this further source of meaning. And since we are experiencing the content as "*out there*"—since it appears to us to be "at a distance"—we must be invoking the general schema of space. Only by placing us both in space and by actively holding the content apart from us in this spatial medium can we distinguish it from ourselves sufficiently to "have" it, to possess it at all as "experience."

Primitive as this sensory experience is, then, it is by no means free of our structuring activity. Definite acts of differentiation, comparison, and categorization enter into it. Indeed, *such acts must be preconditions of its very appearing!* For in order for something to exist for us, it must exist *in some way*; and this "way," then, is the unmistakable mark of our subjective shaping. Any "objective" invariably brings with it the stamp of some "subjective," of some particular direction of interest from which these judgments, identifications, and comparisons issue; and it is thus the *interdependence* of the two that faces us in experience.

We are not ready to pursue the implications of this conception, however, because Realism has not yet finished with its argument. Failing to find its quarry along this structural avenue, it changes its tack and asserts that it is to be found, not in the experience of *static form*, but in the experience of *movement*. We must unhinge from these rigid "things," it now says, and allow our world to expand and flow; and it will be in the fluid dynamic of impressions that then results that we will come upon the raw sensation. It will be in an ever-changing pageantry of form and color that what is closest to the "real" will be found. Accordingly, we make this shift from a spatial to a temporal orientation: with the help, perhaps, of mind-altering drugs, we see if this time we can capture the experience of the pure-sensory.

And indeed, as our hold on the stable "thing" releases and contents begin to slide by, we are presented with a stream of impressions. A flow appears to us that seems devoid of all firmness and structure. Shortly, however, we become aware that this flow is not entirely homogeneous! It is articulated; it presents definite elements of form and color. And this articulation and these elements presume, again, our form-making activity! For only by virtue of judgments of "same" and "different" can even the most minimal distinctions appear. Only by comparing these elements with others we have experienced can we "recognize" anything, can parts of the experience seem in any way familiar. And since the elements of this experience are all connected—since they appear to be taking place "in sequence"—they must be subordinated to the general schema of time. It is *time*, now, that provides the cohesive force that space did before. As before, moreover, this schema is a precondition for the barest sense of an "objective": for if the individual moments of this stream were simply to rise and fall—if each were to sink back into the void again after its appearance—there would be nothing to hold, nothing to set itself over against ourselves as "experience." There would be no way in which experience could "be."

A profound contradiction thus emerges in the notion of a pure-sensory. *The postulation of this type of experience entails the loss of the experience itself!* For by definition, any experience must be "had"; it must be possessed by an experiencing subject that has its own identity and continuity through different experiences. Defining it as "uncontaminated," therefore—purifying it of all traces of the subjective—removes the very hooks by which it may be taken. It makes it impossible for it to come to the subject as "like" or "unlike" other experiences he has had, as connected with anything he has experienced before, as "out there," even, as different from himself. Not appearing as in any way *formed*, therefore, it cannot *appear*. And the idea of it—the notion of a pure-sensory—shows itself to be doomed from the beginning to be—simply—empty.

And so, Realism's doctrine of perception fails. Not only is it not supported in any way by phenomenological analysis, but it shows itself to be riddled with internal contradictions. And with this breakdown in one of its central theses—this collapse of a veritable pillar of this paradigm's system—we are able to return to our previous path and view perception in a constructive light. We need no longer favor it among our mental functions, now, for having lost its role as transmitter of the all-important reality, it has also lost its claim to primacy. And so, we can subordinate perception to that universal instrument of conscious construction, the concept: with Kant, we can define the percept as "a concept with reference to which our presentations have synthetic unity."

This is a construal, however, that cannot help but evoke skepticism. For I have defined the concept as "a rule by means of which things are related." In what sense, then, can a percept be construed as a "rule"? How can it be interpreted as something so abstract, something that is so contrary to the full-bloodedness that is its distinctive quality? We will be able to resolve this problem only by going more deeply into our understanding of conscious activity. When we do, we will see that the rule that informs a content is not always separately determinable: it does not always submit to explicit expression, but may be *a very component of the "thing" itself*. It may be so inextricably bound up with the content, that is, that it cannot in any experiential way be separated out.

In order to fully explain this proposal, however, I will need to bring perception into a wider context. I will need both to go more deeply into the manner in which it functions and bring into our purview a wider range of experiential conditions in which it operates.

4

I will begin by turning to teachings of the Gestaltists, a school in psychology that was active in the early part of the last century. In their investigation of perception, the Gestaltists focused on the "constancies." These consist of processes in which certain features of an object are held constant when they are in fact changing. In matters like "size" and "brightness," for instance, what is actually *different* at successive moments in an object's presentation is rendered in our experience of this object as *identical.* Gestaltists described this phenomenon in terms of the establishment in our functioning of perceptual centers around which certain experiences could be gathered as "the same." In the case of brightness constancy, for instance, this process would make us see as *one* brightness a determinate range of brightnesses that varied from this center. In the case of size constancy, it would cause us to see as *the same* sizes that were in fact different.

Thus, even at this most elementary of perceptual levels, we see again that organization predominates! Far from being simply a passive registration of what is occurring in the environment, perception is active. It engages in a task of *active construction.*

But there is another kind of perceiving as well, one that pervades animal life in general. Unlike the perceiving that eventuates in conscious contents, this kind of perceiving is imageless in character. It consists of response following upon stimulus along pathways that are laid down by instinct and learning (von Uexküll 1909). We experience it ourselves in those multiple everyday actions in which, for instance, we button our clothes in the morning without actually "seeing" the buttons, guide ourselves through a doorway without conscious awareness of the sides we are avoiding, drive to work while "our mind is elsewhere." In this more general animal context, perceiving serves the function of enabling the organism to navigate through its environment in pursuit of its natural interests, all the while learning and forming habits along the way.

Thus we make a distinction between two kinds of

perceiving. It would be a mistake, however, to think that animal perceiving is a precursor of conscious perceiving! Far from being simply a later stage of the former, conscious perceiving is *opposed* to the former; it *goes against* the dictates of stimulus-and-response. For in this newly human direction, the basic impulse is to *stop* the incoming flux with autonomous postulations of one's own; it is to *move away* from the surrounding environment in the creation of an inner environment, a "world" in which the free play of imagination can even better serve the needs of personal will and action. As a result, one's conduct is no longer keyed to the frequency, duration, and intensity of the stimulus; it is based, rather, on the structures that are built on these perceptual postulations.

In this new direction, we need to note, we never actually see what is cast upon the retina. We do not take directly up into consciousness the kaleidoscopic stimulation that assaults our sensory organs. What we see, rather, is these stable constancies. *We see the perceptual constructions that succeed in holding an identity through the sensory tumult.*

This begins the path, then, to further conscious construction. It is a path in which the two factors of *constancy* and *change* are being continually brought into reciprocal relationship. In each of its acts, that is, consciousness establishes some element as invariant and gathers around it others that, by virtue of the concept-principle that it is exercising, "belong." It creates, in short, "transformation groups," determinate sets-of-change through which a certain identity is held.[13]

In conscious life, therefore, we encounter these transformation groups at every turn. We see them appearing first as these perceptual constancies where the groups consist of the different presentations that appear as we approach or recede in respect to some focus of our attention, as the intensity of the illumination changes, as modifications take place in hue. They extend then to "object constancy," to the groups that are formed from the even more disparate appearances that occur when we walk around and look under and over. With a shift in the basis of identity-holding from "form" to "function," then, they move into the sphere of the pure concept; here a category of "dog" establishes a group consisting of all four-legged creatures that bark and are tamable, and another of "vehicle" brings together all the contraptions that function to transport things. Finally, they extend to the widest range of all when, interlocking antecedents with consequences in cause-effect dependency, they succeed in bringing into relationship entire fistfuls of perceptual and conceptual content.

5

Far-reaching as this accounting is, however, it leaves out an important dimension, and this is essential for our complete understanding of experience. For in its most fundamental form, perceiving is imbued with *feeling*; it is deeply rooted in our *affective life*. And when we take this fact into account, we are led to recognize an entirely different kind of experience than the one we have been considering: we are pointed to a kind of world in which perception is not occupied with the creation of objects so much as with the *conveying of emotional valences*. In order to become apprised of this world, we need to bring our focus to the perceiving that takes place in the earliest stages of conscious construction: we need to go to the worlds that are characteristic of children and those who live in mythic societies.

When we do this, we find that those who live in these worlds have an entirely different kind of orientation. What they are presented with is not viewed in regard to its categorial identity as "tree," "person," "dwelling" and the like, but in regard to its character as satisfying or thwarting, benign or malevolent, mundane or awesome (Werner 1961; Cassirer 1953-1957). These are qualities, furthermore, that are transmitted *directly*. In contrast to the kind of viewing that develops later, such characteristics are not seen as "attributes," merely, of already-established objects but are viewed, rather, as the *essence itself* of the experience. Experiences here *speak* their fearsome, soothing, angry messages; in their emotional urgency, they are read as direct communications from elves, spirits, demons, or gods.

This is a world in which a throbbing vitality animates all. It is a world in which, since nothing is categorically fixed and there are as yet no stable "objects," anything can become something else; thus, in animal worship, the members of a tribe can be directly infused with the strength, ferocity, and cleverness of an admired animal. It is a world in which, since no differentiation is being made as yet between what is "subjective" and what is "objective," experiences have an intense immediacy;

they *possess* rather than *are possessed by* the individual. It is a world in which, since the appearance is not yet separated from a something-behind which shows itself through this appearance, everything *is* just as it *seems*; a dream can have all the potency of waking events. And it is a world in which, since there are no firm boundaries, the qualities of the whole flow readily into its parts; possession by an enemy of an individual's tooth, hair or other byproduct can give this enemy control over the individual himself.[14]

And it is a world, finally, in which there are as yet no schemata in which experiences can be placed. Since such forms as "space" and "time" have not yet been developed, experiences cannot be ordered relative to each other. They will occur in a punctate manner, therefore, each disappearing after its occurrence as the individual lapses back again into animal living. Since each experience thus represents a genuine jump in the individual's customary mode of living—since it constitutes a wrenching break into another dimension—it requires greater-than-usual energy; and it is likely to occur, therefore, under conditions of intense emotion. It is when the individual is engulfed in overwhelming fear or amazement, when he is struck by a feeling of great reverence or strong desire, that an "image" suddenly arises; and it is this image then—this "presentation"—that becomes the material for further conscious construction (Cassirer 1946, 83 ff).[15]

6

This construction is carried out by means of ever-expanding organization. In a long and difficult struggle, attempt is made to connect these punctate experiences as they appear and establish amidst their diversity fixed centers of stability. This task requires, however, some kind of tool: an *instrument* is needed in order to effect it. And this instrument is *vocalization*. It is in the ability to produce flexible and repeatable sounds that the human being finds the means for carrying out this organization.[16]

Vocalization holds within it potentials that make it well-suited to this task. To begin with, the voice has a natural ability to express feelings of various kinds, to embody anger or surprise, wonder or delight, pain or grief. Just as directly, the sounds themselves can convey general feeling-tones; they can differentiate the "soft" from the "harsh," the "smooth" from the "sharp," the "incorporative" from the "expulsive" (Werner and Kaplan 1963). The primary need at this point, however, is stabilization. And to effect this, the operative element in vocalization is repetition. By repeating a sound at different times and under different conditions, individuals can endow experiences that are inherently different with a sameness; by uttering on different occasions a *same-vocalization*, individuals can establish a "something" that now carries an identity of its own. In this way, birth is given to "names." And by applying this name-utterance in different settings, this "something" can be repeatedly evoked and the all-important function of recognition begin.[17]

Further stabilization goes hand in hand, then, with advance in the vocalization itself. Eventually these advances gel into a "language," a complete canon of forms for the fixing of determinate meaning-directions. Proper nouns—vocalizations for individuals— are supplemented by common nouns—vocalizations for generalities. Adjective and adverb forms qualify and modify what has been established. Verb tenses permit specification of temporal differences, and a copula opens the door to the complexity of subject-predicate construction. By adding a vowel sound at the end of a person's name, the distance of this person from the speaker—a being-here or a being-there— may be conveyed. And by repeating a syllable in a word, a recurrence may be indicated.

Different societies undertake this formation in different ways, and a diversity of languages thus results. This diversity is indicative, then, of the variety of "worlds" that people inhabit (Whorf 1956). In each of these worlds, a people have come to *live in* their language as in the very air they breathe; they *see* and *think* along the lines that their linguistic forms lay down. Amidst this diversity, however, certain broad movements appear. As elements are evolved for "here" and "there," "near" and "far," "left" and "right," form is given to a modality of space. As elements are developed for "now" and "then," "earlier" and "later," "past," "present," and "future," a general schema is evolved for time. As elements are developed for "one," "two," "several," and "many," a mode is formed for number. As elements are developed for "sources," "effects," "motives," and "consequences," a schema is established for cause. These broader avenues come to represent, then, common modes of world formation: they become *universal parameters* in the shaping of human experience.[18]

7

A unique kind of relationship form underlies all this activity, however, and this brings us to the very heart of conscious construction. Making its appearance as soon as human beings turn vocalization to this unprecedented use—as soon as they elevate what is mere sound into this new and specifically human dimension—this relationship form brings into being the unprecedented factor of *meaning*. The form in question is the symbol; and with it, a peculiar kind of immanence is posited, an interpenetration of two elements that are of different origin and character. We have already encountered this interpenetration in the concept where, in a single entity, a rule that was ideal could infuse material that was concrete; and we encountered it again in the percept where, in a unitary "thing," both a concrete something-seen and the mental judgment, inference, or interpretation that informed it were contained. Revealing itself now in its most essential character, this form manifests itself in the way a mere sound can become invested with *significance*.

It is through the symbol, therefore, that a "given" can be wed with a "not-given," an "appearance" with the "object" it points to, a "fact" with the "assumptions" that underlie and condition it, a "phenomenon" with its "meaning." It is by means of the symbol that the diverse attributes of a thing can "inhere" in that thing, an actual "burgeon" with the virtual, a simple be "filled" with all the possibilities that make it, in the end, complex. *Thus it is the symbol that provides the essential condition for consciousness. Through its mediation, the entire profusion of conscious formations from the most primitive meaning-wholes to the complex systems of mathematics, science, and philosophy are evolved.*

In order to see how this magic is performed, we need to understand the symbol's structure. It is a structure that contains within it two moments, a "sign" and a "signified." And these moments may vary in the degree to which they are differentiated.

In early conscious life, these moments are combined. Sign and signified compose an undifferentiated whole, and no means is given for taking what is immediately given—either the image or the vocalization itself—as indicating something else. In the case of the image, one's view is not being transferred to something beyond that is causing it; rather, the image fills the *whole* of consciousness; it absorbs one's entire interest and attention. And in the case of vocalization, the utterance is entirely integral with the content; it seems not to proceed from the subject but to come back to the subject as conveyer of this content's "soul." It is for this reason that "word magic" arises, and that in the conviction that the word contains within it primitive power, one can believe that "in the beginning was the Word."

The next great step in conscious advance takes place, then, when "sign" is differentiated from "signi-fied." Now the one element in the relationship can "stand for," can "indicate" another. And with this, the image can be interpreted as an appearance that points to something "behind"; a vocalization can "mean" a thing or idea. A new mediateness enters the individual's life with which he can counter the immediacy that imprisoned him before. Distancing himself as subject from what consciousness presents, therefore, he proceeds to develop the great division between "objec-tive" and "subjective"; and progressive specification at these two poles produces—always hand in hand with the development of linguistic forms—multiple "things" at the one pole and an increasingly elaborate conception of "self" at the other.

Two primary modes thus develop within the sym-bolic function, a mode of "presentation" and a mode of "representation." The former accounts for the imme-diacy and concreteness that characterize early con-scious life, and the latter accounts for the mediateness and "objectivity" that succeed it. In the course of this progression, a momentous change takes place in our experience: our initial experience-wholes—each indi-vidual and unique—become transformed into another kind of whole, a *system*; they enter into *complexes of relationship*. These systems arise in near-endless vari-ety, then, in accord with the different areas of interest that become marked out. But whatever the nature of these areas, they share a common thrust: they trans-form experiences as they occur in their unending suc-

cession from a status of self-standing isolation into a
status of mutual contextualization; they endow the
individual experience, now, with *place.*

Throughout this entire activity, the symbol function itself remains hidden. In its role as fundamental
source in conscious construction, it lies itself beyond
visibility. What is visible, in contrast—what comes
into awareness—are its products; and more particularly, this consists—after sign and signified have become
differentiated—of what is *signified.* It is the signified
that presents to us what is meaningful to our will and
desire, our action and knowledge. And it is in the signified that we acquire the direction of focus that makes
us in our mental activity "intend."

For this reason, the objective world appears to us
always to be immediate. It comes to us as "given" as it
stands before us in its concrete multiplicity. How
much the objects of this world are in fact not immediate, however—how much they depend for their very
"being" upon the symbol function—is seen when we
realize that they are never given simply in themselves,
but always *imply* something else. They *hold in their
meaning* other contents, both actual and potential, that
are connected to them along the paths we have previously laid down. It is only by referring our present
content as an "aspect" to other potential contents, for
instance, that we can read it to begin with as an
"object." It is only by referring its "here" to a "not
here" that we can see it as positioned "in space" and
located in front of, beside, or over other objects that
are also in space. It is only by referring its brief and

fleeting "now" both backwards and forwards to a "not now" that we can make it endure and bequeath it with an "identity" that holds through successive temporal moments. It is only by referring it to other contents that are its causes and effects that we can place it in an objective universe at all, that we can understand it as belonging to a great whole whose objects and movements take place in accord with uniform law. *Far from being beheld and dwelled upon simply for itself, now, the immediate content has become transparent to these further events. It mediates the vision into that great spatio-temporal-causal order we call "objective Being."*

8

And science is the enterprise that takes up the task of making exact determination of this Being. Setting the goal of "explaining the appearances," science conceives hypotheses as to still-further objects and events and brings these back to experience for testing. It sets up a shuttle between "theory" and "fact" that enables it to knit a systematic interdependence of the two.

Science cannot proceed very far along this path, however, without initiating certain developments in the symbol-agency. Thus far, the determination of "being" has been effected through the name; it is by naming that "things" first became established, and that ground has been provided for our knowledge-making. As we have seen, however, the content to which this name referred became more and more loaded with reference to other names as it was tied into different axes-of-relation. My simple "tree" at even a pre-scientific level, for instance,

became implicit bearer of all the diverse contents—
"pole," "leaf," "sun," "water"—that could be related to it
through such established conceptual standpoints as
"visually similar," "constitutive part," "causal condition."

Increasingly burdened with these different directions of significance, therefore, these names have
become more and more "abstract." They have
approached the status of *position*, merely, at which
these various axes of relation intersect. Exploiting this
tendency, then, mathematics arises to forge a symbol-
form that *focuses entirely on position*: it creates a *science* of
position, engendering series in which each element is
defined solely by the position it takes in its series. In
the whole-number series, for instance, the number "9"
simply signs the position between "8" and "10." In the
series of circles, a circle of a certain radius signs the
position between circles of shorter and longer radii.

Mathematics thus shifts from the materially weight-
ed "thing" to a model of pure meaning. In its systems,
the density of inner reciprocity becomes such that
each element represents, now, every other. In the
whole-number series, for instance, the number "9"
includes in its very meaning every other position so that
no single one—the number, say, "9834"—can be
removed without changing it in its very "essence."
Thus mathematics becomes the symbol-form par
excellence for science: with the relational facility it
attains, it enables science to transfer its vision into
pure relationship; and this brings into sight the goal of
attaining, through "laws," universal knowledge.

But science is unable to reach this goal directly.

Unlike mathematics, it does not deal with elements of pure form, with systems that are freely constructible, but with the real world, with stubborn, unyielding objects. And these objects, furthermore, cannot be readily serialized in the manner that permits amenability to mathematics. When we try to range them on the basis of their properties, of such qualities as "heavy," "warm," and "quick," they resist; they do not submit to the precise organization into grades and steps that would allow them to be unequivocally placed into sequences of "more and less," "twice," or "half as much."

Science undertakes the construction, therefore, of entirely fresh properties. Developing a new concept-form, it gives birth to "variables" and "parameters." It engenders notions like "mass," "temperature," and "velocity" that will *vary continuously through a range of values.* And since these notions meet the logical conditions that are necessary for ordering into series—since they incorporate such attributes as internal uniformity, continuity, and divisibility into equal parts—they may be organized, now, into the needed grades and steps. They may be "scaled" into the exact intervals that will enable them to be coordinated with the real-number progression.[19]

One further step remains, however, before these parameters can be applied. As constituted, they are "ideal"; they do not exist in the real world of empirical thing and event. Science must devise some means, therefore, for translating the qualities of empirical things into their terms. To this end, it invents "instruments": it selects materials from the physical world that will incorporate these ideal attributes as closely as possible—a rigid rod for length, a column of mercury for temperature, a compressible spring for weight—and, introducing them into the empirical flux, "measures." The readings it obtains on its instruments, then, represent the translation of real events and movements into these parameters.

And so it finally comes into position to undertake the precise sequencing-of-things it desires. By determining that one object weighs 67.1 pounds, another 74.6 pounds, and a third 33.1 pounds, for instance, it is able to exactly order these objects in respect to the parameter of "weight." It is able to construct a domain that yields exact quantitative expressions of its determinations.

But this entire development cannot be completed without drawing into it the notion itself of the "thing." For with these parameters and these operations, science is entering a new conceptual space. And it can remain consistent with the logical qualities of this space only if it redefines the objects that occupy it. Freeing itself from what is directly seen, touched, and felt, therefore, it creates a kind of entity in which *nothing material remains*. It advances a concept for the *"physical body,"* an object that is composed entirely of these parameters. In its domain, now, a "thing" is purely relational in nature: it consists of nothing *but* its length, mass, electrical conductance, and so forth.

And with this, it is able to proceed. Setting up special situations called "experiments," it holds certain parameters constant while submitting others to deliberate change. It makes determination by this means of the functional dependencies that exist among these parameters as their empirical correlates interact with each other in the real world. Giving rise in this way to formulations like f = ma and R = I/V, it reaches its goal of transforming the empirical world into purely mathematical terms; it creates a universe that, in interpretation of our own, can more powerfully than ever before "explain" what happens in our experience.[20]

9

Looking back, now, we see how a striving for stability has gradually brought into being structures that are more and more comprehensive, that have moved us more and more solidly into "objectivity." Along its course, we first drained the vitality of our expressive life into a fixed perceptual structure, a panorama of "things" all spread evenly before. We then made an effort to reach through these things to something still more stable and, emptying their concrete richness even further into an abstract conceptual scaffold, transformed the concrete thing that appeared before us in its inherent luxuriousness—in its lush and colorful leafiness, say—into the "tree" that was merely an instance of something more general. Driving on, we proceeded to create those genetic constructs that, reaching behind these generalities, were even less experienceable; we created concepts for invisible "cells" that would bring our tree into connection with everything that was organic, and "motives" that—discernible only through their effects—connected together diverse individuals. More and more as we proceeded along this path, we found ourselves dealing with things that could not even be sensed; the original richness of our full-bodied presences had given way to a purely intellectual structure. But by means of this structure, we had become increasingly able to stabilize the ever-changing tableau that was continually confronting us.

And this was a progress that was sustained at every point by the symbol activity. When we survey this activity as a whole, now, we see that it contains two fundamental movements. One is directed toward concentration: it condenses what is scattered and diffuse into the unity of a "being," a phenomenological substantiation-of-a-thing. In this way, birth is given to the contents of early expressive life; but it also shows itself later whenever we make effort to reach through things to their essential "center," to grasp the core "character" of something that is vague and diffuse. And so it appears when, faced with some object of great importance to us such as a loved one or pet, we suddenly find arising in us the one word that captures this object's essence, the idiosyncratic "nickname" that evokes its very soul. It appears again in those conceptual acts in which, striving to reach through a multiplicity of ideas to their deeper meaning, we "forge a thousand connections with a single stroke" and suddenly find some new construct or idea lying before. And it appears still again when the artist, trying to reach through his experience of a landscape, a person, a tonal or visual movement to its inner form, succeeds in disengaging the character-of-the-thing and embodying it in his chosen medium. In all these cases, something is made to *stand there* that was not there before; something new is thrust into consciousness as if by a foreign hand.

To formulate something, however, is not to make it intelligible. To bring something into the clarity of impressionistic immediacy is not to bring it into the clarity of understanding. Thus in another direction, we see a movement toward expansion. Now, these presences are drawn into relationship with what is outside; they become subject to placement in encompassing contexts. Shifting its function from *presentation* to *representation*, the symbol activity makes it possible for contents to increasingly "sign" their way into these wholes; and these wholes, concentrated through a name then, may become objects themselves for further contextualization. In this way, an activity of "thought" arises, a constant likening and contrasting, subordinating and superordinating, separating and combining of what we have formed along relationship-lines that we have previously laid down. And this slowly brings to us, then, "understanding"; striving to continually enlarge these contexts, we move towards the goal of a single comprehensive unity, a conception that will succeed in instilling a final "one" into the "many."

Every crystallization of a something-new is thus succeeded by discursive elaboration of its "meaning." Every condensation into a fresh image, object, or concept is followed by its elucidation in terms of what we already have. Intension is followed by extension, and this again by intension. Synthesis leads to analysis, and this to another synthesis. And in this constant ebb and flow, this great sea-tide of the symbol activity, we come to the very heartbeat of consciousness: we lay finger on the living process by which an extraordinary "world" arises, a symbol-skein that spins us into it in measure as it takes on form and being itself.

10

All these considerations give us a platform, now, from which we may return to the fundamental problems. In my critique of Realism, I have shown how the postulates that this paradigm laid down enabled it to provide ready solution to most of these problems, but ran it into difficulty with the question of how our verbal and symbolic procedures play the role they do in our acquisition of knowledge. Further development of these postulates' implications, then, brought to light deep fissures that they generated between a "subjective" and an "objective," an "empirical" and a "logical," a "physical" and a "mental."

Beyond this, however, it has become clear how much Realism possesses a distinct conceptual poverty in regard to the human. "Consciousness," rendered as immaterially subjective, is utterly ungraspable. "Creativity" remains for the Realist a perpetual mystery. The spontaneity that is manifested everywhere in poetry, in architecture, in music, in painting is simply inexplicable. In addition to its purely systematic shortcomings, therefore, Realism shows itself to be deficient in a way that can only be judged to be *moral*: it fails to honor what is distinctively *human*.[21]

With this as the record of the prevailing paradigm, we are all the more impelled to see how the alternative fares. How does a systematic phenomenology resolve the fundamental problems?

1. The question of how our conscious contents come about, of how we come by what presents itself to us, is answered by resort to the symbol function. In its twofold movement toward concentration and expansion, this function gives rise to the entire range of these contents from their most concrete and expressive to their most abstract. The complexities of this production are a matter for continued empirical investigation into the developments that take place in myth and religion, language and art, science and mathematics.

2. The immediacy with which certain of these contents present themselves is sign of the concentrative movement, of the condensation we find in "presentation." Since symbol and symbolized are not differentiated in these contents, the individual has no means for separating himself out as "subject" and placing himself in opposition to what is there. He cannot hold these contents off for objective viewing and experiences them, therefore, with irresistible directness.

3. Interpersonal agreement is explained by reference to the efforts of a society to coordinate its members' individual perspectives and arrive at common ways of viewing. This is carried out first through such mythic practices as communal rituals, then through the agency of language. In both cases, pressure is insistent to "conform"; those who are around continually correct the individual, shaping not only the ways in which

he acts and expresses himself but the articulations he introduces into his perceiving and thinking.

4. Intrapersonal agreement—the fact that I can look away from something, then look back and find "it" still there—is an indication of the object formation that is a central feature of conscious process. These "its" are an achievement of the symbol function of representation: when what is present no longer simply asserts itself but points to something else—when the appearance becomes an "aspect" that is looked through to a central "thing" and then this thing read as an instance of a general category—contents that are inherently different in their form, their spatial position, their time of occurrence become seen as identical. They acquire an "essence" that holds through these different "conditions"; and the path is opened to the "recognition" that constitutes these intrapersonal agreements.

5. Our intersensory correlations, being *experienced* correlations, reflect in another way the ever-present activity of organization. Initially a condition of synesthesia prevails. Contents present themselves as diffuse wholes that contain no indication as to sensory source (Werner 1963, 86 ff). As we begin to apply to experience the question of origins, however, we become able to articulate it into distinct sensory spheres; and these spheres are further organized through coordination of a certain sight with a certain sound, a certain taste with a certain smell, a certain tactile sensation with a visual appearance.

6. The explanation of how knowledge is acquired returns us to the symbol function of representation. It

is this function that creates for us a world "behind" what we directly experience and activates, by means of this world, "explanation." The manner in which this explanation is carried out is itself subject to development (Cassirer 1956). But at no point do we directly take up a reality outside: to "know reality," far from being some dubious leap into the transcendent, is a matter of putting more and more of what we know together; and to "discover truth," far from lighting upon some pre-existing verity, is finding the concepts that will instill into experience a greater degree of coherence.

7. In order to answer the final question, the concern about a descent into solipsism, I will need first to address in greater depth the central concepts of "experience" and "consciousness."

11

When Kant drew our focus away from the outside reality, he offered as the new foundation for our thought the concept of "experience." This concept needs to undergo a change, however, in order to fulfill its new role. Under Realism, "experience" acquires an ephemeral cast; it is assigned to the "subjective" and, in contrast to the solid things of this realm's counterpart, appears as insubstantial and shadowy. With the phenomenological reduction, however, these objective things become themselves moved into the phenomenological realm, and "experience" thus expands to include them. It encompasses *all* our contents, now, the entirety of what we "have." And if this means that the objective itself moves into the shadows, it is nevertheless a shadowland that, in its total envelopment of us and our conscious life, forms the inescapable medium in which all that we see, think, and imagine takes place.

In order to ground the new concept of experience, then, we first move it out from under the aegis of objective-subjective and draw it back into consciousness. Experience is, after all, *conscious* experience. No longer construed as "subjective," it is freed of this long-time stigma and becomes in its character essentially neutral. The predications of "objective" and "subjective" now acquire a new and more limited role: they function to instill distinctions into what composes experience. And since they apply only to its contents, *they cannot be applied to experience as a whole:* such an application would cause them to lose any footing they have in the meaningful.

Similarly, then, with the concept of "consciousness." With the phenomenological reduction, we take up our station "in" consciousness as the arena in which everything that is given is found and the place from which we most securely step forth in our efforts to understand. Since objective and subjective have become categories we apply to our phenomenological contents—since they are a principle of organization *within* consciousness—they cannot apply to consciousness itself: they have meaning only in relation to what consciousness contains.

And these same restrictions obtain, as well, with respect to the other formative agents. In our desire to understand "experience" and "consciousness," we are tempted to apply to them—as we do in other instances in which we are trying to "understand"—such primary forms as "space," "time," and "cause." In this case, however, this application only brings paradoxes. If we should ask, for instance, what "causes" consciousness, we would be able to proceed only by selecting for our explanation some subset of contents *within* consciousness—some set of anthropological, psychological, or neurological conceptions—and thus engage in the folly of trying to reduce a whole to its parts. If we should ask "where" consciousness is, we would not be able to proceed without invoking the category of "space" and, turning again to one of its own contents—in this case, most likely, the percept/concept of the "brain"—trying to locate it in an element it *contains*. If we should apply the category of "time" and ascribe to consciousness the quality of, say, a "stream," we ignore the fact that consciousness is the ground from which all time determinations are developed and that "past," "present," and "future" have meaning only in relation to its contents. Thus, neither "experience" nor "consciousness" can be thought of as being caused, having a place, or occurring in time; and any attempt to apply to them these categories of the *objective* understanding will inevitably engage us in the vicious circle of presuming the very thing we are trying to explain.[22]

In regard to the question of solipsism, then, we see that the problem has, in a sense, evaporated. There is no question now of experience or consciousness falling into "subjectivity"; it is only when we pose objective and subjective as primitives in our system that this threat appears. And when in contrast we consider things more carefully, we see that what was formerly out there is—and has always been—"in the mind." This is a mind, however, that is not opposed in any way to an "objective"; it is a mind that, because of the subjectivistic connotations that have for so long been associated with it, is best represented through the more neutral term "phenomenological."23

And so what was formerly anathema—what in the idea of "solipsism" was at all costs to be avoided— opens now to a productive approach. Reorienting ourselves along these lines, we begin by recognizing the fact that we are inescapably *immersed* in solipsism. The phenomenological reduction ensures this: it stipulates that everything we see, think, or imagine is, in the final analysis, private. As a next step, then, we recognize that, existing from birth as we do "in society," we are in continual interaction with others; we are subject to the influence of those who are around, and this causes us in turn to introduce modifications into our private world. As we bring elements of this world into accord with what is public, therefore, we move in our solipsism—in some measure at least—toward "the common."

"Being in society," however, takes effort. As shown by the long struggle children have to move from their natural egocentricity into a more "civilized" state, it requires of us both willingness and exertion. Various conditions appear, therefore, that result from the incompletion or abortion of this struggle. We see individuals who have insufficiently emerged from their native self-centeredness, for instance, habitually exercising a "me first" attitude; we see individuals who have fallen into a state of depression withdrawing from their engagement with what is around and retreating into their own world; we see individuals who have suffered life-burnout because of their inability to fight any longer the hardships that life brings regressing into focus on their immediate needs. In all such cases, the effort required in "adapting" is given up and the individual becomes content, simply, with his native solipsism.[24]

12

These, then, are the answers the phenomenological paradigm gives to the fundamental questions. At no point in its responses, it is to be noted, does it take resort to an "outside reality"; if it had, it would have been quickly tied back into Realism and the attempt to create an alternative would have failed. But the concept of "reality" nevertheless remains: meaningful in the arenas of both common sense and science—significant in the contexts of both our everyday outlook and our orderly investigation of things—it is explicitly accorded recognition. It must, however, be reconstrued now if it is to remain useful; it must, if it is to be meaningful in the new system, be brought into alignment with our general phenomenological principles.

I have already shown the lines along which this reconstrual takes place. In my previous discussion, I described the role that increasing *determination* plays in pushing our "things" ever further into objecthood.

Something that begins as relatively indeterminate in our perception can, for instance, have the standpoints of "height" and "color" applied to it and be determined to be "tall" and "green." Applying then the standpoint of "object identity" and differentiating it from other tall green objects, we are able to establish that it is a "tree." The standpoint of "species" places it in context with maple, oak, and pine and determines that it is an "elm," and the standpoint of "causal dependency" brings into relationship with it the soil, water, and sunlight it is dependent upon for its growth. At each of these steps, our content acquires greater *definition*; it becomes clearer as to what it is. Thus the "reality" of something shows itself to be a matter of this determination: as we increasingly enrich a thing's contextualization—as we multiply the axes-of-relation into which a thing is placed—it more and more acquires the stamp of the "real"; and "reality" itself becomes the end point in this steady progression.

"Nature" is the name we assign to the domain in which we place the things that we consider to be "real." In order for our experience-of-a-thing to qualify for assignment to this domain, however, it must meet certain conditions: it must be determinable in respect to the three major axes-of-relation. It must, that is, be construable as existing side by side other things "in space," following and preceding other things "in time," and entering with other things into determinate chains of "cause and effect." Then and only then can we say of a thing that it is "in Nature." Then and only then can we say of a thing, indeed, that it "exists."

But this predication of "existence" turns out to be problematic. Since Nature represents for Realism its best estimate as to what constitutes reality, the question of whether something "exists" or not becomes for it an essential judgment. It is a judgment, however, that exerts a distinct bias; for when we attempt to apply it within the field of knowledge as a whole, we find that it makes objects that fall short of the necessary standard uncomfortably ambiguous as to whether they "exist." The psychologist's concept for "manic-depressive illness," for instance, is determinable as to time—it has a cyclic quality; it is determinable as to cause—it has ascribed to it chemical and genetic origins; but it is not determinable as to space—it does not occupy space. Does manic-depressive illness, therefore, "exist"? Similarly with other things we establish in our quest for understanding—the historian's concept for "Zeitgeist," the social psychologist's concept for "group identity," the anthropologist's concept for a culture's "mentality"—do these things "exist"? In all these instances, we are thrown into ambivalence; we are made uncertain in regard to what is a fundamental predication.[25]

13

These ambiguous conceptions, furthermore, are characteristic of the social sciences. They arise most frequently when the object of our knowledge concerns the "human." In the very heart of knowledge, therefore, a fundamental division appears: a rift opens between *Naturwissenschaften* and *Geisteswissenschaften*, between sciences that are "hard" and sciences that are "soft." Within this division, furthermore, a distinct valuation is exerted: the hard sciences are considered to provide us with real knowledge while the soft sciences, falling short of their ideal, are considered to be second-rate.

But these "soft" conceptions are of undeniable value! They unquestionably advance in each of the disciplines in which they have been developed this discipline's understanding! In order to do justice to knowledge as a whole, therefore, a different defining principle than "existence" must be sought. And we find this in the concept of *meaning*. In the new paradigm, questions of "being" are dissolved into questions of "meaning"; the existence of something—a something that is conceived as standing in isolation in an ontological universe—is replaced by this something's *implications*—by the relationships it implicitly holds with the other elements of its concept field. Instead of viewing the particular thing now as an ontological thing-in-itself, we view it as a *functional element in a system*: we regard it with respect to its *meaning within a concept field at large*.

Continuing on this path, then, we go on to identify various "meaning universes" within knowledge in general. Each such universe consists of a group of concepts that are linked by an inner coherence. And each sets a rule for what will be admissible to it as an "object"—for what will be meaningful within its system. In the subdomains that compose the physical universe at large, for instance, such a rule is that their objects be "facts"; they must exhibit such qualities as observability, dependability of recurrence, and measurability. In the subdomains that occupy human realms, in contrast, objects may be admitted that are "idiographic," that relate to individuals' direct experience-of-things; and these need not recur, need not be subject to interpersonal validation, and need not be numerically measurable.[26]

In the course of knowledge-making as a whole, then, various meaning universes arise as different areas become marked out for methodical investigation. And since the overriding goal in knowledge-making is to achieve a final unity of understanding—is to create a single comprehensive frame in which every object and every event can be seen as having lawful place—a major task becomes the *integration* of these universes as they independently form. This is accomplished through the development of concepts that "underlie" those that are at work in two or more domains. By means of such concepts, a deeper focus is attained, a more profound perspective from which derivation can be made into each. A certain development in the concept of the "atom," for instance, enabled investigators to bring into integration the independent universes of chemistry and physics; by means of the organizing principle that this concept now embodied, they were able to make statements regarding events that took place in both these domains.[27]

In the new paradigm, therefore, we are able to avoid the bias that is introduced when we attempt to make determination as to the "existence" of things.

But there is another side to this transition as well. In our knowledge-making in general, the phenomenological paradigm puts before us multiple "worlds" rather than a single dominant world; it faces us with a diversity of meaning universes rather than a single "outside" against which we, as subjects, are set. And since all these worlds arise from application of the symbol function—since they are generated through specific steps of symbolic formation—this paradigm brings us directly into the realm of the human: it places us immediately in the arena of *human construction*. Our former preoccupation with the "physical" recedes, then, and the enterprise that devotes itself to understanding this domain becomes but one in a general circle of enterprises, each of which contributes to the edifice we call "knowledge." The supreme task becomes, then—instead of determining what in the final reckoning "exists"—determining what the systematic place of each is in the circle as a whole.[28]

14

Before returning to the theme of "perspective" in my final chapter, I will briefly take up two objections that are commonly made to the phenomenological standpoint. Each of these often stands in the way of serious consideration of this standpoint, and additional elaboration may clarify what about them is still problematic.

The first concerns the impression we have of the "solidity" of things. In everyday life, we experience many things as possessing a material tangibility. They are "solid"; they are "concrete." How, then, do we account for this tangibility? What causes this impression of solidity? With Samuel Johnson, we kick the stone and it hurts: How can a mere "phenomenon," a mere "content of consciousness," cause this acute pain?

In reply, we begin by recalling the new status in our system of "objective" and "subjective." Experiences can be viewed as "merely" phenomenal only if they are standing under this polarity. Assigned then to the subjective side, they are viewed as insufficiently of the character of a *fundamentum*, as too insubstantial and ethereal, to deserve portrayal as "solid." When instead we posit *experience* as primary and relegate objective-subjective to the role of principle operating within experience, "touchability" becomes simply a *kind* of experience; it becomes an aspect-of-things that, when integrated with other aspects that are visual or auditory in character, yields this characteristic "solidity."

We see, furthermore, that this is a characteristic whose special use occurs in the earlier stages of conscious construction. It is when the individual is emerging from a mythic into a reality-oriented mentality that it becomes important to segregate what is "real" from its antithesis in, for instance, illusions or dreams. As further advance is made into objectivity, the importance of tangibility diminishes; and science casts it aside entirely when it replaces criteria that are direct-experience-based with criteria that are system-based. Now, it is not the solid trees, animals and people of our experience that represent what is "really out there," but the "atoms," "genes," and "quarks" of scientific hypothesization.

And so, the real becomes shifted into that very "abstractness" that before was its antithesis. Tangibility gives way to what is purely "intellectual." As we have seen, furthermore, this system-based principle—this principle of *organization*, of bringing under a single aegis what is isolated and disparate—is operative when we turn back to our concrete experience-of-things as well. It was only by organizing different appearances into a unity that we were able to possess our primitive "things" to begin with. And it was by means of further organization that we could integrate our sense of touch with some of these things to give rise to this quality of "solidity."

The second question concerns the implications of finding ourselves so phenomenologically confined. The consequences of this total immersion in a private world seem so indigestible at first sight that it can well discourage further consideration of the phenomenological viewpoint. Does such an immersion mean, now, that there is *no real world* beyond our own? Does it imply an eradication of the entire universe that lies outside and around us, that existed before we came into being and will continue to exist after we are gone? Does it involve doing way with the ultimate source in which everything, including ourselves, arises and has its existence?

The answer is that the reduction in no way obligates us to give up the notion of a real reality, an *an sich* that is quite independent of our conscious activity. On the contrary, we have every reason to continue to view ourselves as living in a real world of things and events, as subject to outer circumstances whether these be cataclysmic in nature or mundane, as ensconced in a wider universe that lies all around. The "critical" point so essential to Kant's position, however, is that *this* reality, being forever beyond the horizon of experience, lies outside the bounds of what we can meaningfully inquire into, think about, and understand. Our statements in regard to it, therefore—drawing as they must on conceptual structures we have developed for experience—will always be metaphorical in character: they will consist in figures of speech that we have hurled into the dark, merely, from our station in the light.[29]

When we speak of the *an sich*, then, it is by necessity in the terms that our spatial, temporal, etc. templates supply. We say that the universe is "outside" and "around" us, that it continues "before" and "after" us in our temporal existence, that it is the "causal source" from which all animate and inanimate things arise, that it is "objective" in character. Once we have made such statements, however, we have no foothold for further inquiry; we are given no basis on which to conduct any kind of investigation that would yield understanding. In order to arrive at such understanding, we must move back into the world of meaning: we must turn to that *meaning domain* whose character and dynamic it is the concern of the phenomenological paradigm to define.

Chapter 4

PERSPECTIVES IN
EVERYDAY LIFE

*"For it is not a question of what we see
in a certain perspective, but of the
perspective itself."*
—Cassirer, *Myth and Language*

1

In my discussion thus far, I have sought to establish that we can never know things as they actually are, but only as we see them to be. Exploration of this "seeing" then led us to its vehicle and expression, the perspective; and perspective-taking showed itself to be present, in turn, in all conscious activity. It manifested itself in perception in our having to occupy some particular standpoint, always, in order to come by what we see; it manifested itself in our thinking in our being thrust into a partial view of things whenever we applied some concept or concept group; it manifested itself in our conscious action—in action that was not simply reaction or the habituated product of learning—in our needing to apply some perspective in order to give this action direction. Perspectives thus constituted the very fabric of experience. They could not in any way be surmounted; and they could be abolished only at the cost of abolishing experience itself.

Such a conclusion would seem to cast us irretrievably into an ocean of relativism. If the reality is unattainable, we must think, we will lose all anchor in our seeing and thinking. If the "truth" can never be known, one idea must be as good as the next. And this is the conclusion, indeed, that is frequently drawn in our postmodern era where every absolute is renounced and our beliefs in such absolutes replaced with disquiet and uncertainty.

In my analysis, however, I went further. Continued investigation of perspectives showed that they possessed an inherent capacity for augmentation. By establishing a "deeper" perspective, others that were more limited in their reach could be brought together and integrated into one that was more comprehensive; and this new perspective, then, could become subject to further integration. Thus the possibility was established of continuous progress. And if "reality" and "truth" were not themselves directly graspable, they could be held out as something to be ever more closely approached: they could in good faith be *reached* for.

Thus this augmentation, this constant combining of perspectives that are already present into new ones that are more comprehensive, became a prime characteristic of conscious activity. In my discussion, I focused on this activity in the area of knowledge-making where it became the basis for scientific advance;

but it shows itself in other areas as well. We see it in political life, for instance, when a nation develops an overall "doctrine" that—still perspectival in nature— gathers into it a number of previous stands it has taken in regard to various national and international issues; we see it in social life when a group congeals from the views and principles that its members hold a distinctive "philosophy"; we see it in our personal life when we form from a variety of opinions or beliefs a "political position" or a "belief system." When in common parlance we speak of "gaining perspective," we refer to just this effort to rise to a more inclusive view. And when we speak of "keeping perspective," we refer to avoiding a slide into a view that is more one-sided and partial.[30]

Continuing, then, I showed that perspectives have a special kind of structure. This consisted in a unity that held within it two moments, a standpoint from which things were viewed and the "something" that then became visible from this standpoint. In intimate linkage, a subjective position was tied to objective material. And so, whatever became objectively "there" inevitably pointed back to subjective factors: it necessarily entailed interests, intents, and values that were being exercised by the individual.

This same structure showed itself in another conscious element, then, the concept. Here a rule—a certain way-of-ordering—would bring into being as its extension a range of objects that were so ordered. In this way, a rule of similarity could be employed to posit a concept for "house" that would then make certain kinds of structure stand forth in experience. A source concept for "Jim" could bring into its extension all the different visual presentations, verbal expressions, mood manifestations, and actions I experienced in relation to this particular friend.[31]

In their inherent nature, then, concepts necessarily became *instances* of perspective. They always put a certain light on things. They always exerted some kind of "spin" on experience in general.

But a further factor showed its presence, now, one that was essential to both perspective and concept. This was *language*. In order to become established, both perspective and concept depended upon the word; both required a verbal embodiment that could be reproduced in order for these elements to be held. Thus, we were brought into the universal presence in conscious activity of the symbol; and it was the *symbolic function* that showed itself to be the source, finally, from which conscious life in all its aspects flowed.

This opened to our understanding, then, the peculiar kind of relationship that had so often baffled thinkers in their investigation of conscious functions, the unique *interpenetration* in these functions of things that were entirely dissimilar. In perception, this interpenetration manifested itself in the puzzle of how something that was objectively seen could incorporate into it a mental judgment, inference, or interpretation. In conception, it manifested itself in the puzzle of how an abstract principle could infuse and affect concrete material. And in linguistic usage itself, it was manifested in the greatest enigma of all, the puzzle of how something so arbitrary and trivial as a *sound* could become invested with *meaning*. Other relationship-forms would come to light in the analysis of objective construction; but these—"space," "time," "cause," etc.—invariably invoked, if only implicitly, the element of meaning.

With this, then, we gained purchase on the genesis of the great domains of human expression. For the structure of the symbol showed itself to be—consistent with that of the perspective and the concept—a unity that contained in it two moments. In this case, these moments were the "sign" and what was "signified." And by attention to the degree to which they were differentiated, we were able to uncover the preconditions for the various kinds of "world" that people created; we gained access to the dynamic that brought forth in all its diversity the wonder of "culture."

And so we saw that, when these two moments remained undifferentiated, the stage was set for the mentality that evidenced itself in the worlds of mythological societies and children. Since what was subjective was not yet differentiated in these worlds from what was objective, experiences pressed in on one with compelling immediacy; they could not be held off in objective viewing and fluidly changed, accordingly, with the fluctuations that took place in subjective feeling. Imbued with a spontaneous and unpredictable quality, experience in these worlds acquired a magical character and such practices as prayer, ritual, and sacrifice arose to structure and regulate it.

With differentiation of "sign" from "signified,"

then, the new function of *representation* could form and the conditions become set for objective viewing. The common sense world in which we have "real things" all laid out objectively before us could develop and a steady march undertaken into knowledge. In these two great modes of "presentation" and "representation," therefore, the agencies that brought into being the entire panoply of cultural forms were disclosed. Myth and religion, art and poetry, mathematics and science testified to the extraordinary potential that the symbol function contained.

2

When we bring our focus down to the individual, now, we see this drama being played out on a more intimate scale. Early stages in the individual's development are ruled by "presentation." Positioned as he is in the posture of naïve Realism, this individual has no awareness of a subjective component; his implicit belief is that "the way I see things is the way they are." Since he doesn't yet recognize the fact of perspective, he tends to become locked into particular ways of viewing things; and he manifests, therefore, a certain rigidity, an inability to adapt very readily to the changes that are going on around him. Ensconced at this stage in his native solipsism, he believes that the world is just as he has it.

As he begins to differentiate subjective from objective, then, he becomes aware of perspective. He is able to take into account the fact that others may see things differently than he. Representing these others' views to himself, he begins an inner dialogue. And correlatively, the operating principle by which he guides himself changes from "the way I see things is the way they are" to "the way I see things is simply the way I see them." His initial presumptiveness drops away and, cognizant now of the "otherness" of those who are around him, he is able to contribute more productively to his society's dialogue.

And it is dialogue, indeed, that is the heart of "society." It is by constantly exchanging perspectives with each other that individuals knit a fabric of "community." It is by opening to the views of others that individuals become able to establish beyond their own interests and intents something that is common. At any given moment in the life of a society, this dialogue will have a history: it will carry forward perspectives and dialogue that have taken place in the past. And since individuals inevitably differ in their perspectives, it will also contain dissension: conflicts will arise that need to be resolved through continued exchanging.

The integrity of a society thus depends upon the sustaining of its dialogue. When a society falls under authoritarian rule and this dialogue is interrupted, the delicate fabric that is "community" is torn. And while this rule may seem to have the beneficial effect of dampening the dissension, it is in fact destructive: it produces regression to that "jungle" state in which the society's members turn to pursuit of their individual interests. Deprived now of their motive for communal effort, they fall back into their native solipsism.

These contingencies operate as well, then, in the

smaller arena of interpersonal interaction. When an individual believes that "the way I see things is the way they are," he is prone to exercising a kind of dictatorship. He thinks that there is only one way to see things—*his* way—and is accordingly led to impose his views on others. With awareness of and tolerance for "perspective," on the other hand, he is able to see himself as part of a communal net. He acquires the ability then to participate in the dialogue that is constitutive of democracy.

3

The analysis of perspective has made us aware of the intimate link that exists between a perspective and its embodiment. In my discussion, I have focused on this embodiment as it takes place in language. Here, we have seen, words *establish* perspectives; they each cast things for us in a certain way. In general, therefore, the vocabulary and linguistic structures that a society possesses determine how its members will view things. Providing ready-at-hand perspectives, they present the rails along which the perceiving and thinking of these members ride.

There are times, however, when preestablished structures do not suffice. When we try to give utterance to something that lies deeply within, when we are at pains to capture some novel perception or feeling, when we are newly coming to understand something for which we have as yet no adequate formulation, we are under necessity to *create* our vehicle. We are obliged at such times to bring a perspective forth, as it were, *ex nihilo.*

The clearest illustration of this process is found in art. Endeavoring to give expression to what is vaguely "inner," the artist must often construct a fresh vehicle from the beginning. He must *create* the lines and shapes with which he paints, the physical medium in which he sculpts, the sequence of movements from which he composes his dance. Working and reworking his material, then, he keeps on until this vehicle reflects his intent; he posits and erases, arranges and rearranges, composes and recomposes until the material faithfully transmits the inner. In a process of mutual determination, form and matter at such times are thrown into a cauldron, there to interact with each other until some "being" emerges; and the struggle continues until a work is put before us that embodies his unique perspective.[32]

This process may take place as well, of course, in the domain of language. In order to give expression to something new, the speaker or writer must take structures that are pregiven and mold them afresh. He must twist and turn these structures until they express his meaning. This "meaning," however, does not preexist the material! On the contrary, it emerges into existence only *with* the material. A perspective and its embodiment, meaning and its vehicle, form and matter "become" together in reciprocal interaction.[33]

In daily life, we shift between the preformed and the new. Much of our commerce with others—as well as our own thinking—rides along the rails of the already-formed; and this may descend, of course, into cliché or kitsch. But when an urge is present to capture some unique feeling, to give form to some fresh impression, to clarify what is only dimly seen, we must perforce wrench into being something original: we must undertake a struggle to lead from the depths what has hitherto been unsaid.

And similarly, then, in the domain of pure conception. Involving here an interaction between "hypotheses" and" facts," the creative process consists of a bringing forth of the two together. The facts receive their form from the theoretical light that is being put forth. Usually thought of as pregiven, they are in fact "turned" constantly to bring them into alignment with different possible interpretations.[34] Facts and hypotheses together form a whole; and it is through their mutual adjustment that this whole attains systematic unity.

But what has been preformed may enter this process as well. When a psychotherapist faces the task of understanding a new client, for instance, he must gather as his "facts" the ongoing verbal and nonverbal expressions that, in interaction with him or her, he observes. In addition to this, he is concerned to obtain what data he can from evaluative instruments that have been used and the historical record of previous actions and events that have occurred in his client's life. He tries, then, to make of everything a coherent pattern, to give it the unity that will provide him with "understanding." In pursuing this goal, he has at his command a number of preestablished formulations for the types and dynamics of "personality."[35] These are but way-stations, however, in his progress toward that deeper center that will express what before him is unique; as perspectives that have already been codified, they fail each and in their sum to give adequate representation to what about his client is *particular*. He moves back and forth between facts and hypothesis, therefore, making conceptual stabs at this center until he attains the perspective that brings the entirety into a whole; and he continues until everything he knows about his client is endowed with coherence and intelligibility.[36]

4

I will turn at this final point in my exposition to contextualization of the ideas I have been discussing in trends that are current in present-day philosophy. In this postmodern era, philosophy has been moving towards various of the positions I have been presenting. It has been increasingly explicit in its criticism of Realism and the objectivism that this paradigm propagates; it has turned to language as a key ingredient in all cognitive life; it has affirmed the inevitability in human functioning of "historicity," of handed-down perspectives in what we say, think, or do. More and more, it has elevated the time-honored discipline of "hermeneutics": it has recognized the ever-present role that *interpretation* plays in human thought and expression (Mueller-Vollmer 1985; Ricoeur 1981); and since interpretation involves the application of some partial slant, view, or "take" on things, it has recognized—implicitly at least—the fact of "perspective."

But a curious pall hangs over these efforts. With

objectivism's demise, the specter of a relativism has emerged that is essentially trivializing, that renders everything that one arrives at transient and contingent. And the goals that before were enlivening—the "search for truth," the "determination of reality," the "quest for the ultimate nature of things"—have become suspect: interpreted as the simplistic beliefs of a bygone era, they have all evaporated. "Reality" has disintegrated into as many versions of it as there are individuals to apply to it perspectives (Goodman 1978); "truth" is scorned as a well-meaning but idealistic illusion of our forebears; and the theorists of today foresee only endless deconstruction, the peeling back of layer after layer in what has already been created without place for a counterbalancing *construction*.

What seems missing in this modern outlook, then, is the presence of an overall frame. What is lacking is a "paradigm," in short, that will invest these different movements—in the absence, now, of Realism—with meaning and direction. In proposing for this role the phenomenological paradigm I have been discussing, I have shown how a standpoint can be attained from which "construction" is seen as the *heart*, actually, of conscious functioning. Such essential elements in this functioning as the "perspective" and the "concept," furthermore, are subject to continual augmentation; though fated always to be relative, they may progress to higher and higher levels of universality. "Reality," therefore, retains its meaning: while demoted from its standing as a fixed external source, it becomes indispensable, now, as a living goal. And "truth" in turn is similarly preserved: while dethroned from its high position as something absolute, it maintains its place as necessary standard in our constant effort to separate wheat from chaff.

There seems little reason to despair, then, of our overall direction. If there is no other certainty as we look ahead, there will always be the certainty of *human creativity*. There will always be the irrepressibility in art, in literature, in science—in every field of human endeavor—of *originality*, of the ability to over and over surprise us with the fresh and wonder-filled. Like a sudden reversal in the magnetic field, then, what has been negative can switch to positive; what has been felt as an unwelcome restriction from the standpoint of "knowing reality," "establishing the truth," "arriving at the ultimate nature of things" can turn instead into liberation. This is the liberation that comes with awareness at long last of both our limitations and our possibilities. It is the liberation of attaining solid ground, finally, on which to build.

NOTES

1. One must mention in this regard Husserl's concept of "essence," an attempt indeed to advance a notion for what is elemental in conscious activity. An essence is a structure that lies behind and informs the direct phenomena of experience (Spiegelberg 1984, 95-97; Moran 2000, 134-136). To my mind, however, there is little to distinguish it from the ordinary concept which also, as we shall see, functions actively in conscious organization. This interpretation of the concept's function, however, depends on overcoming the traditional doctrine of "abstraction," the idea that the concept is simply a lifting out of what a group of things have in common; and although Husserl was in process of taking this step (see de Boer 1978, 154-156), he was unable to wean himself entirely from a substantial orientation. His conceptualization tended in the end to resort to some kind of real *fundamentum*—a tendency that seems indicated in his choice itself of the term "essence."

2. See Wilkerson (1976) for extensive documentation of the frequent ambivalence that Kant was still having regarding his "noumena" and the accessibility of the real.

3. For a more detailed exposition of these points, see Merleau-Ponty (1983/1942). His conclusion: "It is

not the stimuli . . . which determine the contents of perception. It is not the real world which constitutes the perceived world" (p. 88).

4. The similarity of this formulation to one that is well-known in Kant's first *Critique* is apparent (Kant 1929/1781, 93). What was for Kant a necessary feature in a relationship between two "faculties" (those of "sensibility" and "understanding"), however, becomes seen now as testimony to the inextricability of two poles in a *single* element, the perspective.

5. I use the word "perfect" here because the child's construction of the object is more complicated than it first appears, involving a number of steps. See also Bower (1979).

6. The fact that indication and recognition do their work quietly—the fact that they act, so to speak, behind the scenes—would seem to lend them a certain mystery. It might even invite us to dip at this point into mysticism. In reality, however, these two operations are but instances of the symbolic function; and when I describe this function more fully later, I will be showing that the reason for their invisibility is that, since the symbol activity lies at the heart of conscious construction, it cannot *itself* be visible. Visibility is achieved through its products, through the perceptual and conceptual contents that it produces; and as the spring from which everything that we "see" flows, it remains itself in the dark.

7. Strange as such a notion may seem, it was already being advanced in all clarity by no less a figure than Hermann von Helmholtz. More than a century and a

half ago, Helmholtz was writing: "[Experience can give us different sensations] if we should move our eyes or our bodies and view the object from different sides, touch it, etc. The totality of all these possible sensations comprehended in a total presentation is our presentation of the body. . . . although contrary to ordinary usage, such a presentation of an individual object is already a concept, because it comprehends the whole possible aggregate of particular sensations that this object can arouse in us when viewed from different sides, touched or otherwise investigated" (*Handbuch der physiologische Optik,*" quoted by Cassirer 1910, 292-293).

8. My construal throughout this discussion differs from one that is current in philosophy and that places the weight of knowledge, not on concepts, but on propositions. According to this latter view, there are two kinds of proposition, those that express beliefs about things and those that provide justification for these beliefs; and it is the combination of these that gives rise to knowledge (Rorty 1979, 131 ff.). Furthermore, justification propositions come about through communal effort, through conversation and dialectical exchange; and knowledge becomes at heart, therefore, a social-linguistic enterprise.

Without minimizing the importance of social interchange in the achievement of knowledge, I feel that not enough recognition is given in this view to the role of the concept. It is in the concept that we come into touch with the actual creativity—and the struggle—that is involved in creating knowledge. The concept of "atom," for instance, was subject to development through many centuries before it could achieve its inherent fruitfulness; when this happened, it posited a structure that could draw into determinate relationship the diversity of chemical elements. The drama— the excitement, the frustration, the triumph—that imbues knowledge-making is lost, I feel, when the focus is on second-stage propositions.

Innumerable examples of the illumination that concepts bring can be found in any field of inquiry. A personal memory is the sudden enlightenment that came to those of us who were working with adolescents when Erik Erikson introduced his "identity" concept (Erikson 1950; Erikson 1968). What before had been wrapped in obscurity—what had been a confused jumble of mood changes, impulsive behaviors, volatile feelings, and directionlessness in this particular age-group—suddenly became intelligible; what had been chaotic became ordered. Established now as a meaningful stage in the overall course of human development, the "identity period" became instrumental in the definition of other stages in adult life (Sheehy 1976; Levinson 1978).

9. Needless to say, this is not the "ideality" of various Realistic systems that are denoted as, for instance, "idealism" or "rationalism." In these latter cases, some super-sensuous entities—ideas, laws, spirit, God—are still being postulated as the ultimate Being, and the essential thrust of these systems toward a final "reality" is being preserved. In contrast, we are discussing a *functional* ideality, an ideality whose entire meaning is

exhausted in its activity, in its effecting.

10. The diversity of ways in which things are perceived under different conditions of age, affluence, etc.
was the subject of lively exploration during psychology's "New Look" period (Bruner and Krech 1950).
Since the findings were not in line with Realistic
expectations, however, they were marginalized and
had little influence on psychology's subsequent course.
There have been few more striking examples of the
way in which thinking in a discipline gets snapped back
into accustomed molds by a prevailing paradigm—no
matter what the "evidence" may be that lies nakedly
before one's eyes (Kuhn 1970).

11. One may refer here to interesting experiments
along these lines in Cantril (1950).

12. Helmholtz struggled with this problem throughout his distinguished career and ended by submerging
it in his famed notion of the "unconscious inference"
(see Boring 1950, 308-311). Here as in other instances
of intellectual travail, the "unconscious" becomes a
convenient burying ground for one's systematic cul-
de-sacs. By assigning entities and mechanisms that
arise from faulty systematic principles to a realm that
is by definition impenetrable, one can believe that he
has "explained" them.

13. Cassirer has illuminated the way in which, at
the very highest level of conscious functioning, the
mathematical theory of groups gives precise expression to this process. In the theory of groups—in "this
universal instrument of mathematical thought"—
transformation groups are established in which an

identity is held through determinate variations in some mathematical element. By establishing a "projective" standpoint for geometrical figures, for instance, the different forms of "point," "straight line," "circle," "ellipse," "parabola," and "hyperbola" can be brought into essential identity (Cassirer 1945/1938).

14. Poets try to recapture the quality of this earlier world and renew for us the intensity of feeling that it contains, the colorfulness that so naturally imbued our experience when we were younger. Indeed, some authors argue that we should return to this earlier mode of living and restore the nature-consciousness that is characteristic of indigenous populations. This is a consciousness which we lost in our steady march into civilization, they contend, and became preoccupied with controlling, manipulating, and exploiting what is around (Abram 1996).

In addition, there is a trend among modern thinkers to focus in their conceptualization on "lived experience." Husserl and Heidegger, among others, make the "Lebenswelt" the ground of their philosophy; and in psychology, a similar "phenomenological" trend resorts to the "life world" as the basis for a more meaningful kind of research (Wertz 1999, 151). We have seen, however, that "experience" is not the simple thing it is often thought to be. In even the most primitive of circumstances, it consists of both the real and the ideal, of the at-hand and the not at-hand, of what is given and what is created. And we have seen as well that there is everywhere present in it an element of construction. In their idealization of this "living" form of experience, these authors seem to under-appreciate, not only the presence in it of creative activity, but the intense human need to move beyond it and transform it through conceptual development in a striving for "understanding."

The "primitive" is always there, of course, no matter how far we think we have advanced into civilization. We are most likely to experience it when we come into some extraordinary circumstance—when we feel sudden terror, for instance, or threat to our survival. Finding himself caught in the San Francisco earthquake of 1906, William James tells how he uncharacteristically resorted to prayer; Joan Didion, in grief over near-unbearable losses, describes the ways in which she succumbed to magical thinking (Didion 2005). In the political arena, return to this stage and its "primitive" emotions becomes a deliberate goal of leaders who try, for instance, to bring a citizenry into readiness for war: they attempt to arouse and guide these emotions by such means as incendiary slogans and patriotic rituals designed to induce in their citizens a state of unthinking regimentation (Cassirer 1946).

15. This line of reasoning leads to the positing of image-making—of "imagination"—as a primary human function, one that cannot be explained by any other process. Indeed, images show their self-standing status in fantasy and dreams where they are produced—in contradiction to traditional theories regarding the need for sensory origins—in the absence of sensory input. Further evidence of this independence

is given by those who are congenitally deprived of sensory channels. Helen Keller, for instance, blind and deaf from an early age, gives eloquent testimony to the detail and "color" of her world: "The silent worker is imagination which decrees reality out of chaos" (Keller 1908, 14).

Imagination creates not only images, of course, but entire "spaces." And it is here more than in anything that is strictly visual that its true power lies. It is the power of projecting through and beyond anything that is immediately before us a virtual dimension, a space in which it can have free play. In this way, a Shakespeare could arc out worlds that are more vital and "real" than our own; a musician can tirelessly riff on a basic theme; a scientist can thrust through the familiar universe to another that, near-inexplicably complex, "explains" it. In our own personal lives, imagination is surely our most precious possession; and the cruelest loss is its suppression, perhaps extinction, at the hands of caretakers and educators who are overly dominating in their "guidance" (Hardy 1973).

Since the image contains no differentiation as yet between an objective and a subjective, it is only when we have crystallized this distinction that we are able to advance to the "percept" per se. Now images can acquire the ability to "intend"; they can "point to" things that we take to be outside them. From our newly objectivistic standpoint, then, we relegate the image itself to the "subjective" where it is to inhabit fantasy and dreams. This transition from an image-oriented to a percept-oriented stage is not accomplished without difficulty (see Merleau-Ponty 1963); and it would be a mistake to think that, along the way, we have lost the former's qualities. On the contrary, this earlier stage continues to be available to us and, with its lack of differentiation between a subjective and an objective—with its inherent "murkiness," its absence of anything that is readily verbalizable—holds special potential for creative formation.

And from this standpoint, the magnitude of the transition that language effects comes into sharp relief. "Man is relieved by words of the need to make 'pictures' of things" (Cassirer 1996, 215). For in order to raise ourselves above the constant flow of pictures—of images—that we have in early conscious life, we need to inject into this flow something new; we need to undertake a new direction of construction, one in which we impart to these images a *function*. The function is representation, and it is effected through the "name." When an image is named, it is no longer lost amidst the particulars, arriving and as quickly disappearing as it is replaced by another, but enables us to stand back and obtain through it a "view"; it transfers our vision to other images that may be drawn into relationship with it by means of one or another rule. In cases of brain damage where this function is lost, we see the individual regressing to the "concrete"; he cannot respond to a picture by calling it a "knife," but returns instead to the practical world of motor action and says it is "for cutting." Unable now to see beyond what is immediately before him, he cannot bring into view other knives in consideration, say, of what "kind" of knife it is or think of possible uses it might have other than cutting.

16. It is understood that this vocalizing activity takes place in a context in which individuals and societies are already well advanced in their ability to deal with the environment. The sensitivity of the "savage" to his surroundings—the acuity of his vision and hearing, the sophistication he has developed in hunting and fishing—is well documented. This sophistication does not of itself, however, imply consciousness.

17. There is a well known period in children's development in which the child suddenly becomes preoccupied with learning the names of things (Stern 1923, 162 ff). If this "Namenshunger" is looked upon not merely as a standard "learning" phenomenon—an acquisition of adult-formed denominations-for-things—but an essential stage in the child's structuring of his world, we can understand better its compellingness: it represents a magic key that opens to him, now, that "gorgeous fever" from which will issue all the personal and cultural riches that the human capacity for consciousness contains.

18. See Cassirer (1953-1957) for a detailed study of the way in which this entire development proceeds. As Cassirer's investigations make clear, it is a development that is rooted in and evolves from the early constructions of myth.

19. Galileo, who is to be credited with initiating this parametric movement, thought that these valuable new concepts diminished our ordinary experience. By the side of such entities as "force," "acceleration," and

"mass," he said, such common qualities of this experience as color, size, and heaviness became, now, "mere names." They were but "secondary qualities" in comparison with the power these concepts had to bring us to the very heart of nature.

20. This movement can be followed in psychology where this discipline, eager to emulate the physical sciences, forms a similar kind of object. Needing to prepare itself for the activity of measurement, psychology gives rise to a concept for "subject." It creates a notion for its disciplinary object, that is, that retains nothing of the characteristics of the living and breathing person who enters its lab. Whether this person be male or female, old or young, healthy or handicapped is irrelevant unless these are among the variables on which it is measuring: possessing no "being" apart from these variables, the subject becomes the point, merely, at which they intersect.

This transformation has far-reaching consequences, of course, for psychology's knowledge-making. It puts into jeopardy, in fact, its entire enterprise. For in jumping so quickly into this parametric skeleton, in turning its back on the rich qualities that the human being possesses, it leaves unfinished its initial task, the articulation and definition of these qualities. There is good reason for a science to be occupied in its first stages with "observation": it needs at this early point to acquaint itself with all the diverse forms that its subject takes in our experience of it so that it may taxonomically order them. By this means, it arrives at its first discipline-specific concepts, the "types" that bring these forms into organization. It is from this base, then, that it goes on to develop its higher-order concepts, including those that function to "explain." By passing over this activity in its urgency to reach the stage of measurement, psychology deprives itself of the foundation it needs in order to achieve a *meaningful* knowledge (Hardy 1988, 87 ff).

21. This moral poverty shows itself nowhere more clearly than in the fate the human sciences suffer under its aegis. In fealty to Realism's objectivism, these sciences degrade the human being to a shallow "behavior." They designate as central to their scientific object—as the feature in terms of which all its other features are to be understood—the one that is the most superficial. Taking on the garb of "behavioral science," then, they become obsessed with exact, if empty measuring. And the outcome is the loss of any compass that could orient and guide them. Helpless now before anything that is humanly "inner," they lose their ability to maintain their integrity: they inexorably fragment into multiple unrelated initiatives (Hardy 2000).

22. For further elaboration of these points, see Cassirer 1910, particularly 309-310.

23. At this point, the Realist is likely to think that this apparent exaltation of "mind" satisfies his long search for a *fundamentum*. "Mind" will be what is ultimate, now, what will supersede any other conception as to what constitutes the "real." Going on in this rationalistic vein, then, he will speculate about Absolute Mind; or turning to the related concept of "Self," he will posit as his *fundamentum* a

Transcendental Ego or Transcendental Subjectivity. "Mind" and "Self" continue to be, however, concepts! As with any concept, they call for investigation of their development in the life of consciousness as a whole, simply, and definition of the contexts in which they arise and possess their meaning.

24. Reflection of the degree to which an individual has made progress in this adaptation is given in the manner in which he conducts his discourse. When this falls into an "expressive" mode, he habitually gives voice—sometimes at length—to what he is feeling and thinking; he takes little account of others who may be around and of what they may be thinking. When it takes place in an "interactive" mode, in contrast, it is directed specifically toward these others; it consists of a back and forth in which this individual makes a statement, waits for a response, then responds to this response. The indication in the former is of relative self-ensconcement, and in the latter of a more vital engagement with others and recognition of the existence of their perspectives.

25. Along these lines, we may finally lay to rest, perhaps, the perennial question "Does God exist?" Few examples can be given of a concept that so egregiously exceeds the necessary determinations. By definition, "God" does not occupy space, has no cause, and is eternal. Given this indeterminability, then, "exist" can have no foothold; and the question whether God exists is ensured of being as long-lasting—as little bound by time—as its subject itself.

26. The experimental psychologist S. S. Stevens

usefully brings measurement down towards these idiographic kinds of object. By delineating different levels
of measurement according to the degree to which they
satisfy certain logical conditions, he is able to define at
the lowest of these levels a "nominal" action in which
different things are brought together under a general
category. They acquire by virtue of their membership
in this category equality; and in turn, this permits their
numeration and the comparison of their category on
the basis of this numeration with other categories.

One has to be careful, however, in regard to this
"equality." When things take up membership in a category, they do so as *instances*. And the equality that is
at issue here is a long step from the equality that, at the
most advanced of these levels, is expressed in the
mathematical equation.

27. A similar kind of integration has long been
sought in the case of Realism's mind-body split. Here,
too, two distinct meaning universes confront us, one
incorporating objects and events that are physical and
physiological in nature and the other objects and events
that are "mental." The customary approach is to consider these universes to be two domains of "being" and
to seek the real-world elements in the one that materially "produce" the phenomena of the other. It is to
find—most commonly—some physiological process in
the brain that "causes" events that are mental.

If, instead, we construe the task as one of finding a
concept which, "underlying" these two domains,
mediates derivation into each, we quickly realize why
this Realistic effort must fail. We are pointed to the

fact that both these universes consist inherently in *concepts*; and since these will ultimately be "mental" in nature—since they belong to the generally phenomenological domain—the attempt to explain the mental in terms of the physical/physiological devolves into a vicious circle. The "explanation" will have already incorporated the mental in any subset of concepts it selects.

28. Thomas Kuhn (1970) has done much to further this humanization of the sciences. In his study of scientific paradigms, he points out how fragile, in a way, any paradigmatic perspective is, how prone it is to being replaced by a new perspective. Not that this change—this "revolution"—is arbitrary: on the contrary, a kind of logic controls it, a predictable course from the presence of one or more indigestible anomalies through stiff resistance to change on the part of an "old guard" to the boldness and creativity of those (usually younger) who give birth to the new paradigm. Science under Kuhn acquires a distinctly human cast: it is not directed in its development by objective facts so much as by fallible human beings who are striving to give order and meaning to such facts.

The reduction that takes place here in the prominence of a single enterprise (physics) also opens to us the interactions that in fact occur between cultural forms that are normally considered to be separate. In psychology, for instance, artistic creation comes into play in the formation of the "case studies" that provide it with its initial material. It is in these individual portraits that the discipline first begins to organize the bewildering array of human personality-forms into careful depictions; and the more these portraits achieve standards that are purely literary in quality— the more they are exact, pithy, and evocative in their characterization—the more successfully they serve as ground for the extraction of the "traits" and "types" that will advance the discipline to its next level (Hardy 1988, 98-102).

In another direction, it has been noted how mythic thinking frequently infuses a science's first formulations. Each entity that it posits seems at the time of its discovery to be some kind of august "being," some creature that, godlike in its potency, has been successfully tracked to its lair. Only gradually as this mythic aura fades is this entity recognized to be a *concept,* merely, standing ready for interrelationship with other concepts and placement in a system.

29. In this connection, it is important to emphasize that the ontically real brain is indispensable for the mind just as the ontically real external world is indispensable for our seeing. Without an external world we would have no perception, and without a brain we would not have a mind. But this doesn't mean that we can in either of these cases *build our understanding* of the latter from the former: such an attempt will always run up against the category jump that will make any explanation fail; and however refined our understanding of the brain and its structures becomes, this jump will never be evaded.

30. One sees the operation of perspective on this kind of grander scale in instances of falling in love and

religious conversion. In both these cases, it is as though one has acquired (in the words of William James) a "shifting of [one's] centres of personal energy" (James 2002/1902, 181). The all-too-different directions—the changing interests, concerns, pursuits, emotions—in which one has been pulled before have undergone a gelling now by virtue of the center that this new standpoint provides; and the uprush of feeling that accompanies these events is due, in part at least, to the relief of having acquired for one's self a new unity and purpose. As is so often the case, the standpoint itself in such reorderings remains unworded: it is its correlative object, the loved one or God, that absorbs and fills consciousness.

31. Since "similarity" provides the basis for the formation of our classes, it is by far the most frequently used of our ordering principles. The flexibility we have in applying it, however—the creativity with which we can judge things as "the same"—is generally unrecognized. In his typical manner, the Realist will turn such judgments into discoveries of actual similarities-of-things in the real world; he is seeing, he thinks, a configuration that is being presented by Nature. When this configuration is composed of events that take place in time—when what is "same" appears, that is, as a temporal simultaneity—he may consider it to be a mystical "synchronicity," a concatenation-of-things that expresses the universal spirit and is laden with a cosmic message (Tarnas 2006, 50ff).

What goes unrecognized in these hypostases is the function of the perspective in bringing into conjunction just *these* aspects of human experience. Provided the right standpoint is found, anything can be read as "similar" to anything else; and the psychologist makes use of this fact when, in a standard test of intelligence, he requires the examinee to find a way in which, for instance, "enemy" and "friend" are alike. When a perspective is applied, it automatically brings into view what "fits." And the hidden action in these real-world "discoveries" is always the establishment of some subjectively-generated point of view.

An art as much as a skill, perspective-taking varies widely in its manifestations. The rapidity with which it can be conducted shows itself nowhere more clearly, perhaps, than in the way a group of teenagers can shift in their conversation among different facial expressions, bodily postures, and voice intonations as they role-play their way through various virtual perspectives. At the other extreme, the individual who narrow-mindedly believes that "the way I see things is the way they are" persists often in perspectival rigidity; he conveys by means of his posture, facial expression, and voice intonation the authority of just *his* perspective. The ability easily to adopt another's perspective—to "put oneself in another's shoes," to "understand where one is coming from"—is needed equally by the help-giver and the salesman. And in humor, the delight often comes from being caught by surprise by an unexpected perspective.

32. Picasso remarks in this regard: "When you begin a picture you often make some pretty discoveries. You must be on guard against these. Destroy the

thing, do it over several times. In each destroying of a beautiful discovery the artist does not really suppress it, but rather transforms it, condenses it, makes it more substantial. What comes out in the end is a result of discarded finds."

33. This reciprocity is given pithy expression by a female character in a novel when she complains: "How can I tell what I think till I see what I say?" (Forster 1927, 152). Equally pungently, Merleau-Ponty states as he examines the relation of language and thought: "Speech, in the speaker, does not translate ready-made thought, but accomplishes it" (Merleau-Ponty 1962, 178).

34. Kuhn remarks regarding science: ". . . theories do not evolve piecemeal to fit facts that were there all the time. Rather, they emerge together with the facts" (1970, 141).

35. A common source for these preformed perspectives is the categories that are put forth in the *Diagnostic and Statistical Manual of Mental Disorders* (1994). A good deal of controversy has surrounded the use of such categories. On the one hand, they invoke the human degradation that Kierkegaard expresses in his aphorism "Label me and you negate me"; and indeed, whether applied to individuals or to entire societies, they can reflect an ingrained attitude of the kind that stereotypes Italians, for instance, as "lazy," African-Americans as "inferior," women as "fickle." On the other hand, however, they possess an unavoidable legitimacy. Since it is through categories that we take our first steps into understanding—since it is by

finding some way in which to *typify* an individual or a group that we are able to discern the common thread that runs through diverse features—we cannot eschew categorization without turning our back on knowledge itself. From this purely knowledge-making standpoint, then, the harm in attributions of the kind given above lies in their taking of a category as representative of the whole of what one is looking at: ignoring the complexity of the human—blocked, perhaps, by innate prejudice—one is failing to go on to look for further predications.

36. My formulation throughout here is consistent with that of the "hermeneutic circle." Its process is well described by Ast (see the translation of his *Grundlinien der Grammatik, Hermeneutik und Kritik*, Landshut 1808 in Ormiston, G. and Schrift, A. 1990; see also the reference to Ast in Bontekoe 1995, 18ff).

REFERENCES

Abram, David. 1996. *The spell of the sensuous*. New York: Vintage Books.

Ackerman, Diane. 1991. *The moon by whale light*. New York: Vintage Books. (Quotation is on p. 131).

de Boer, Theodorus. 1978. *The development of Husserl's thought*. Boston: Martinus Nijoff.

Bontekoe, R. 1996. *Dimensions of the hermeneutic circle*. Atlantic Highlands, NJ: Humanities Press International.

Boring, Edwin. 1950. *A history of experimental psychology*. New Jersey: Prentice-Hall.

Bower, T. G. R. 1979. *Human development*. San Francisco: W. H. Freeman.

Bruner, J. S. and Krech, D., eds. 1950. *Perception and personality: A symposium*. Durham: Duke University Press.

Cantril, Hadley. 1950. *The why of man's experience*. New York: Macmillan.

Cassirer, Ernst. 1923. *Substance and function & Einstein's theory of relativity*. Translated by W. and M. Swabey. New York: Dover Publications. (Originally published in 1910).

————. 1945. Reflections on the concept of group and the theory of perception. *In Symbol, myth, and culture: Essays and lectures of Ernst Cassirer 1935-*

1945. Edited by Donald Verene. New Haven: Yale University. (Originally published in 1938).

———. 1946. *The myth of the state*. New Haven: Yale University Press.

———. 1946. *Language and myth*. Translated by Susanne Langer. New York: Harper Brothers. (Originally published in 1923).

———. 1953-1957. *The philosophy of symbolic forms, Volumes I-III*. Translated by Ralph Manheim. New Haven: Yale University Press. (Originally published 1923-1929).

———. 1956. *Determinism and indeterminism in modern physics*. Translated by O. Theodor Benfey. New Haven: Yale University Press. (Originall published in 1936).

———. 1996. *The philosophy of symbolic forms, Volume IV: The Metaphysics of Symbolic Forms*. Translated by John Michael Krois. New Haven: Yale University Press. (Quote is on page 231).

Dennett, Daniel. 1991. *Consciousness explained*. Boston: Little, Brown.

Diagnostic and statistical manual of mental disorders. 1994, Fourth edition. Washington: American Psychiatric Association.

Didion, Joan. 2005. *The year of magical thinking*. New York: Alfred A. Knopf.

Erikson, Erik. 1950. *Childhood and society*. New York: W.W. Norton.

———. 1968. *Identity, youth and crisis*. New York: W.W. Norton.

Forster, E. M. 1927. *Aspects of the novel*. New York:

Harcourt, Brace & World.

Goodman, Nelson. 1978. *Ways of worldmaking.* Indianapolis: Hackett Publishing Company.

Hardy, Anton. 1973. *Guidance vs. exchange in human relationship.* Guilderland, New York: James Publications.

———. 1988. *Psychology and the critical revolution.* Guilderland, New York: James Publications.

———. 1998. The mind body problem. *Contemporary Philosophy* 20:36-38.

———. Psychology's fragmentation: The philosophical dimension. (unpublished manuscript).

James, William. 1902. *The varieties of religious experience: A study in human nature.* (Centenary edition, 2002). London: Routledge.

Kant, Immanuel. 1929. *Critique of pure reason.* Translated by Norman Kemp Smith. New York: Macmillan. (Originally published in 1781).

Keller, Helen. 1908. *The world I live in.* Edited by Roger Shattuck, 2003. New York: The New York Review of Books.

Krois, John. 1987. Cassirer: *Symbolic forms and history.* New Haven: Yale University Press.

Kuhn, Thomas. 1970. *The structure of scientific revolutions.* Chicago: University of Chicago Press.

Levinson, Daniel. 1978. *The seasons of a man's life.* New York: Knopf.

Merleau-Ponty, Maurice. 1962. *Phenomenology of perception.* Translated by Colin Smith. London: Routledge. (Originally published in 1945).

———. 1983. *The structure of behavior.* Translated by

Alden Fisher. Pittsburgh: Duquesne University Press. (Originally published in 1942).

Moran, Dermot. 2000. *Introduction to phenomenology.* London: Routledge.

Mueller-Vollmer, Kurt. 1985. *The hermeneutics reader.* New York: Continuum.

Ormiston, G. and Schrift, A., eds. 1990. *The hermeneutic tradition: From Ast to Ricoeur.* Albany: State University of New York Press.

Piaget, Jean. 1954. *The construction of reality in the child.* Translated by Margaret Cook. New York: Basic Books. (Originally published in 1937).

Ricoeur, Paul. 1981. *Hermeneutics and the human sciences.* Trans. John B. Thompson. Cambridge: Cambridge University Press.

Rorty, Richard. 1979. *Philosophy and the mirror of nature.* Princeton: Princeton University Press. (Quotation is on p. 12).

Sheehy, Gail. 1976. *Passages: Predictable crises of adult life.* New York: Dutton.

Spiegelberg, Herbert. 1984. *The phenomenological movement: A historical introduction.* The Hague: Martinus Nijhoff Publishers.

Stern, William. 1923. *Psychology of early childhood.* Translated by Anna Bartwell. New York: Holt & Co. (Originally published in 1914).

Stevens, S. S. 1951. *Handbook of experimental psychology.* New York: Wiley.

Tarnas, Richard. 2006. *Cosmos and psyche: Intimations of a new world view.* New York: Viking Penguin.

Werner, Heinz. 1961. *Comparative psychology of mental*

development. New York: Science Editions. (Originally published in 1948).

Werner, Heinz and Kaplan, Bernard. 1963. *Symbol formation: An organismic-developmental approach to language and the expression of thought*. New York: John Wiley & Sons, Inc.

Wertz, Frederick. 1999. Multiple Methods in Psychology: Epistemological Grounding and the Possibility of Unity. *J. of Theoretical and Philosophical Psychology* 19:131.

Whorf, Benjamin. 1956. *Language, thought, and reality*. Cambridge: The MIT Press.

Wilkerson, T. E. 1976. *Kant's Critique of Pure Reason: A commentary for students*. Bristol: Thoemmes Press.

Uexküll, Jacob von. 1909. *Umwelt und Innenwelt der Tiere*. Berlin: Springer.

INDEX